WISDOM

FOR OUR

TIME

by

**DANIEL
WARREN
GUDEMAN**

**Quality Life Publishing Company
San Diego, California**

International Standard Book Number: 0-962-2416-0-1

Published by Quality Life Publishing Company
ll727 Invierno Drive
San Diego, California 92l24

Cover Photo Credit: NASA

Printed by
Sanders Printing Company
Post Office Box 160
Garretson, South Dakota

(605) 594-3427
Toll Free 1-800-648-3738

ACKNOWLEDGEMENTS

Quotes and excerpts from *Great Books of the Western World* are reprinted by permission from Encyclopaedia Britannica, Inc.

Quotes from *The Dialogues of Plato,* translated by Benjamin Jowett, are reprinted with permission from Oxford University Press.

Quotes from Hegel's *Philosophy of Right,* 1821, translated by T. M. Knox, are reprinted with permission from Oxford University Press.

Quotes from St. Thomas Aquinas's *Summa Theologica,* Benziger Publishing Company. Reprinted with permission.

Excerpt from Wolfgang von Goethe's *Faust: Parts One and Two,* translated by George Madison Priest, 1941, Alfred A. Knopf, Inc. Reprinted with permission.

Quotes from Immanuel Kant's *The Science of Right,* translated by W. Hastie, T. & T. Clark, Edinburgh. Reprinted with permission.

Raymond B. Cattell, *BEYONDISM Religion from Science* (Praeger Publishers, New York, a division of Greenwood Press, Inc., 1987), pp. [42, 50, 61, 66, 68]. Copyright (c) 1987 by Praeger Publishers. Reprinted with permission.

Reprinted with permission from Raymond B. Cattell, *A New Morality From Science: Beyondism,* 1972, Pergamon Books, Ltd., England.

PREFACE

It is a great pleasure to write this foreward to Dan Gudeman's novel treatment of important social and personal problems of which we are all aware. His aim and treatment are novel in that he builds around quotations from famous people over the past two or three thousand years. It is surely to be expected that by now human wisdom has said, pointedly, all that needs to be said about human behavior. Plato, Aristotle, Plotinus, Descartes, Mill, and others frequently condensed years of acute observation into a few words. Dan Gudeman has culled some of the sayings most applicable to our time and has dwelt on their particular meaning for our society and our personal development.

The arrangement is in chapters each covering some topic of present-day concern—equality, morale, libertarianism, knowledge, and so on—that are handled by the current newspapers we read with far less depth and perspective than the wisdom of the ages warrants. His treatment is naturally discursive in organization, because of limitations of space, and the unreadiness of the average man to face a "heavy" systematic treatment. But, nevertheless he treats all aspects and provokes the reader's readiness to think on fundamentals commonly neglected. I venture to hope and believe that this modest book will constitute a revelation to many, and a social re-arousal of important thinking in our jaded age.

– Raymond B. Cattell

INTRODUCTION

A people which takes no pride in the noble achievements
of remote ancestors will never achieve anything worthy
to be remembered by noble descendants. — **Macaulay**

We are becoming more and more shallow because we do not
read. No longer curious and absent the benefit of the wisdom of
the ages, our very survival is threatened. This work clearly
demonstrates that the rise of the great nation, America, was not
an accident.

Many present-day viewpoints, often considered to be profound, diminish when held in the light of the collective wisdom
of the ancients. Not only does this work acknowledge pearls of the
past, it merges the best thoughts of those who have gone before
us with one of the finest thinkers living today.

For the classics, the writer read and studied Encyclopaedia
Britannica's *Great Books of the Western World* (54 volumes), in
addition to studying history, philosophy, psychology and theology. The wisdom and maturity of Dr. Raymond B. Cattell provide
a cutting edge which is representative of the best of modern
thinking. Seven years of conversation with Cattell evolved into
this synthesis of classical and modern thoughts, which provide
guidelines for standards of life worth living.

Without speed reading, the creation of this small book could
not have been accomplished in one lifetime. The practice of
selecting and typing thoughts in excess of 500 pages of abstracts
over a period of ten years, made this final draft possible. Of the
500 pages, a selective distillation of ten pages are contained
herein.

The writer's aim is to revitalize thinking; agreement or disagreement with the many viewpoints is secondary. May the reader take one sentence at a time; this little volume is filled with more thoughts of consequence than we presently are able to fully grasp. Nonetheless, let us courageously rise to the challenge of competition and cooperation in a global world whose brake pads have worn thin.

– Daniel W. Gudeman

CONTENTS

CHAPTER ONE

IS WISDOM MODERN?

The proper realm for wisdom pertains to relationships among human beings; it is patently false to limit wisdom to making shrewd financial investments, to securing a well-paid job, to "successfully" cheating one's neighbor and/or government, or in contributing to the maintenance of the ignorance of associates. Our generation is in the process of falling out of the grace of wisdom; hence, the challenge to define wisdom is bewildering for many. Conversely, Berlin's Max Planck Institute is presently engaged in studying wisdom. Let us step back 2,400 years and permit the ancients to give the first lesson.

> And this is wisdom and temperance and self-knowledge
> –for a man to know what he knows, and what he does not
> know.   **PLATO 1**

The tragic downfall of our age is a lackadaisical attitude respective to that which we do not know. The certainty with which many claim correct answers to the simplest of questions is painfully embarrassing in the face of inaccurate and misleading responses. The embarrassment lies not in ignorance but in the conviction that completely wrong answers are correct. This gap in perception is not about issues and questions which can not be resolved (for example, discussions about God and life after death); the gap pertains to ignorance of basic facts about life and realization of global changes. Provincialism and selfishness perpetuate a narrow mind incapable of grasping the significance of larger issues. A case in point is a woman, whom the writer knows, who prides herself in having read no other book than the Bible during the past fifty-five years. Yet she would not independently acknowledge that her life is considerably more pleasant due in great part to the existence of millions of different kinds of books since Gutenberg.

Every generation is vain enough to believe itself more advanced than former generations. Cultural vanity is no different. Considering the ancient wisdom of the Greeks and Romans, no new generation can claim to be more advanced than its predecessors except in the realm of technology. At the precise moment in time when the modern world stands in the greatest need of wisdom, we have neglected the habit of cultivating it. This neglect is evident when observing the prevalent disdain and rejection of ancient wisdom, aggravated by our failure to create wisdom for our time.

It seems there are no limits to technological breakthroughs (since the dawn of the Industrial Revolution to the present, advances have continued uninterrupted); yet, how do we explain the resistance to progress in human cooperation at a time when modern conveniences ease our lives? Could there be a trade-off: the greater our opportunity to avoid chores or purchase amenities to reduce them, the less interest in developing an integrated life exemplified by personal excellence and harmonious coexistence? It is possible to enjoy the use of an expensive automobile, to luxuriate in the finest living environment supported by fat dividends and returns on investments, but . . . how many people are in a position to show concern for the mounting divorce rate, the relentless pursuit for distraction, the tendency toward isolation, the passion for shamming (superficiality) and the shallowness of interpersonal relations? Thousands upon thousands of citizens brandish masters and doctorate degrees, knowing deep in their hearts how ill-equipped they are in honest and meaningful human interactions; moreover, many don't seem to care.

Ours is a generation which loves the vicarious stimulation of Superbowl, boxing championships, MTV, video game centers, Hollywood scandals and government soap operas. The appetite for distraction and the drive to devour life get in the way of pausing long enough to consider seriously where we will end. For example, have you ever met a proprietor of several large properties who is perpetually short of cash? This individual immediately reinvests all profits to acquire more and more properties, never once questioning whether there are additional ways to expend energy. Likewise, middle, upper middle and upper classes acquire many of the latest contraptions while rarely challenging themselves (in a serene state of mind) with the question, what is quality living (which we are proud to recommend to our children and grandchildren)?

> They that deliver themselves up to luxury are still either tormented with too little, or oppressed with too much; and equally miserable. **SENECA 2**

By contraptions I mean the presently endless, and still to be invented, ways for amusing ourselves. The relentless pursuit of pleasure does not increase wisdom. It is possible to seek out and respect wisdom without sacrificing pleasure.

Let us take a hard look at how we spend time and examine the thoughts in our minds. It becomes apparent that wisdom is left to the dust of the past. Considering our blatant disregard and aversion to "history," it ought not come as a shock that wisdom is similarly scorned. History and wisdom are closely related in that wisdom limits the reoccurrence of failure by keen observation of past errors and actions. Its aim is to avoid repetition of the same mistakes in the present and the future; hence, wisdom requires the passage of time. Our generation deludes itself into thinking that comforts and conveniences of present-day living are far more valuable than the insights and wisdom of preceding generations. The delusion is so successful that we no longer choose to be bothered with a level-headed investigation of the past with the intent of rediscovering relevant thoughts and wisdom.

The implication of Descartes' "I think, therefore I am," goes deeper than is readily evident. In seeking its deeper meaning we not only discern the boundaries of our thinking but become aware that habitual thoughts delineate the limitations of our potential. It takes time to acquire wisdom; it takes even longer to create wisdom. With Gutenberg's forerunner of the printing press (1453), radio, TV video machines and satellite communication, the possibilities for honoring and promoting wisdom to her exalted position have never been greater. It defies the imagination to consider the society and culture former civilizations might have created with the availability and advantageous use of printing and television. We presume to be a great civilization but in view of the present neglect of wisdom, how great are we? Would Jesus cast us into outer darkness for failing to fulfill the principle: to whom much is given, much is required? It can not be debated that we have been given the most and we have the greatest opportunity to create a New Renaissance. Only one reality can stop us dead in our tracks: the failure to advance the quality of human interaction, and a regression caused by the refusal to re-establish the significance of wisdom. Expansive and proper use of intelligence follows on the heels of honoring wisdom, particularly the kind of intelligence which increases knowledge of social harmony. An old truism states: mankind must learn through suffering what s/he refuses to learn through reflection. There is no wisdom without reflection.

An understanding of history is inevitably important. A common attitude echoes one student's disgust with the study of history: "Why study the dates of wars and dead men's lives?" It is true that a typical approach to the study of history is similar to that of a drunkard striving to drive correctly in that both fail to integrate past experience. A useful study of history extracts relevant information with the aim of applying lessons learned, in the present and the future. A view of history which focuses primarily upon facts and figures is burdensome. We must value and increase the richness of psychological content in the social sciences and their relevance on the basis of immediate practical value, if academia is to awaken interest and wholehearted participation of students.

> It is a sad fact that though the people of Europe have been studying Greek life for at least five hundred years they have profited little by the lesson left upon record— as little as the Greeks themselves. The moderns appropriated from the ancients what gratified the taste, but gave hardly any practical attention to the things that would have made life a thousandfold more worth living.
> **C.W. SUPER 3**

Not only has Europe failed to profit from the record of ancient Greek history, America also incorporates less and less ancient wisdom which adds to the quality of life. A mysterious formula seems to operate: the greater the opportunity for creating a New Renaissance, the more elusive the apprehension and capitalization of that possibility.

During the 1950's corporate America appeared to be indomitable. As corporations grow in size, the fat of incompetent middle and upper management increases. As the heart of a body is stressed by excessive fat so does the heart of a nation weaken when individuals are rewarded for fraud, dishonesty and plain and simple laziness. Since World War II, the <u>average</u> Japanese has labored twice as hard as the average American. This provides some explanation for the present difference in the stability of our respective economies. A vigilant nation recognizes that competition becomes keener as technology increases. Viewpoints which fail to accept this are slumbering. The creativity which drives technological discoveries is not equally distributed throughout the world; the presence or absence of creativity depends upon natural resources, cultural drive and standards, minimal governmental interference combined with fair governmental regulation (which provides a sense of stability), and intelligent application of blood, sweat and tears. Beyond a shadow of doubt, America had the greatest opportunity to set standards for quality living for all of the world following World War II.

> ...for this is the law of nature and of God that the superior shall always overpower the inferior. In what? In that in which it is superior. **EPICTETUS 4**

Americans are averse to thoughts pertaining to superiority and elitism. We are unable or unwilling to see value in these concepts and experience discomfort when they are discussed. Is this wise at a time when other leading countries (Japan and West Germany) recognize the significance of that which is superior and are doing everything possible to develop and promote superiority? America recoiled from promoting individual excellence by equating superiority and elitism with gross abuses of power, absence of character and aberrant selfishness—the kind of selfishness which disregards the well-being of fellow citizens. By responding negatively to the term "superiority," we lose out on superiority of character. Let us face this fact: superior character and inferior character exist. Better and worse live. Best is a reality which changes as people and time restructure environments. What is best today can quickly disintegrate and become the worst tomorrow.

Our age despises genetic reality, yet the greatest geneticist of all time was Jesus.

> Even so every good tree bringeth forth good fruit; but a corrupt tree bringeth forth evil fruit. A good tree cannot bring forth evil fruit, neither can a corrupt tree bring forth good fruit. Every tree that bringeth not forth good fruit is hewn down, and cast into the fire. Wherefore by

their fruits ye shall know them.   (Matthew 7:17-20) 5

A tree which "bringeth not forth good fruit" is an inferior tree alongside the tree which does bring forth good fruit.

> Souls vary in worth; and the difference is due, among other causes, to an almost initial inequality; it is in reason that, standing to the Reason-Principle, as parts, they should be unequal by the fact of becoming separate.
>
> **PLOTINUS 6**

Socrates in a conversation with Cebes:

> ...but I am confident that there truly is such a thing as living again, and that the living spring from the dead, and that the souls of the dead are in existence, and that the good souls have a better portion than the evil.   7

Socrates believed that our deeds follow us not only in this life, but also into the future. Moreover, good souls have an advantage over evil souls. Who can say that good souls and evil souls are the same?

Christianity places great emphasis upon faith. The book of Hebrews says that faith is the evidence of things not seen. Not a single person living has seen the Greek empire of the fifth and fourth centuries B.C., yet with faith and intelligence, it is possible to reconstruct the kind of world that then existed, based upon historical accounts and knowledge of Pericles, Socrates, Plato and Aristotle. These individuals possessed a depth of thinking which our age can not boast. The Greek era has come and gone, an era which comprised superiority and inferiority.

A sobering and relevant point of wisdom is the acknowledgement that a spirit of loving-kindness does not rule the world. The entire point of this section: the superior survives and endures. If this is untrue, we would have ceased to exist long ago.

We have access to the wisdom of the ancients; it lives and lives to our embarrassment. America is a country of citizens who are quick to accept ready-made beliefs and too lazy to develop independently derived personal convictions. One aspect of wisdom is knowing what to choose and knowing what to reject.

> It would, indeed, be dishonorable to mankind, if the regions of the material globe, the earth, the sea, the stars, should be so prodigiously developed and illustrated in our age, and yet the boundaries of the intellec-

tual globe should be confined to the narrow discoveries
of the ancients.   **FRANCIS BACON 8**

A persistent reflection upon the philosophy of the ancients
results in incredulity (with a long look at today's world), when we
consider that superior conclusions on human behavior and government have been available for more than 2,400 years. Worse
yet, modern men and women have not advanced those conclusions. Even Francis Bacon refers to the best of the ancients as
"narrow discoveries." His view does not detract from the wisdom
of the ancients; it merely emphasizes how little we have done to
further the wisdom of the ancients.

> Those incapable of thinking gravely read gravity into
> frivolities which correspond to their own frivolous Na-
> ture.   **PLOTINUS 9**

Plotinus believed that we discern value only through the development of mature thinking (in contrast to a pedestrian response concerning serious issues). For example, we are taught
that communism is the enemy. What does this mean? Communism is a form of economy whose primary focus is the community
first and the individual second. America became a great community of people by focusing first on the individual and second, on the
community (state). The downfall of communism occurs when significant numbers of people think and behave similarly. When
millions of people watch the same stupid television programs,
when students across the nation develop less and less academic
skills, when our culture rewards creative and valuable individual
contributions less and less, we are on the verge of a <u>community</u> of
people who are not significantly different one from another. Our
challenge is to advance beyond preprogrammed responses (frivolity). All forms of government which restrict or limit the development of true individuality are the enemy. It is easy enough to
know the limitations and pitfalls of communism; it is far more
difficult to face our collective ineptitude.

Wisdom is the cumulative effect of Truth. A noisy mind (one
accustomed to seek distraction) can neither receive nor develop
wisdom.

> When we are alone and quiet we are afraid that some-
> thing will be whispered in our ear, and so we hate the
> silence and drug ourselves with social life.
>   **NIETZSCHE 10**

Not only are we mad with social life, we madly pursue the accumulation of material goods above and beyond what is necessary to live comfortably. We need to be reminded that <u>overindulgence</u> with materialism is as detrimental as is deprivation of material goods. The danger inherent in exclusive attachment to materialism is death of mental cultivation—which equates with cultural deterioration. America now has millions of citizens (financially secure) who are failures—people who live undetected in their failure while hiding behind money and material goods—but not for long. Evolution in time eliminates that which lacks substance (this includes entire civilizations). Life is precious; to account for life strictly on the basis of balance sheets and statements of account is indefensible.

The meaning of "freedom" requires the support of wisdom. For some, freedom is none other than an opportunity to pursue frivolity; in other words, a life burdened with boredom, dullness and emptiness. Freedom is a two-edged sword which either paves the way to a New Renaissance or leads to the poverty of enslavement.

> A plausible profession this in words, but really unmeaning and delusive, and the greater the disguise of freedom which marked it, the more cruel the enslavement into which it was soon to plunge us.   **TACITUS 11**

Without a major turnaround by 1990, America is destined to lose the status of a first-rate nation. Where do we begin to put our country back on her feet? Take our drug problem. Enforcement is one approach but very difficult when individuals in many walks of life, from the bottom to the highest echelons (including those whose job it is to enforce anti-drug laws), are dependent upon drugs. Something is seriously lacking in the quality of life of an individual who is attracted to habitual drug use. Prohibition of alcohol did not work; those with whiskey thirst took to the hills and distilled spirits. Do we legalize drugs? No. Our challenge is to remove the inordinate <u>desire</u> for drugs and chemical substances. No societal problem is wholly overcome until <u>individual</u> and responsible thinking are stimulated.

The American school system requires revamping. Significantly disturbed pupils can not develop mentally until they acquire minimal emotional stability. Without a beginning foundation of emotional stability and character development, efforts aimed at other areas are counter-productive and increase frustration for the student. Life is a ruthless teacher and the relegation to special classrooms is not nearly as harsh as drug and alcohol rehabilitation centers and jailhouses, or living on the street for that matter.

> Wisdom lies in human action which possesses both intellectual and ethical orientation; and the promotion of such wisdom is the task of education everywhere and at all times. **D.E. LAWSON 12**

What have we learned about wisdom? ONE: It takes centuries to create wisdom. TWO: Wisdom exists and is recorded for our benefit, but there is a major catch—we are required to expend tremendous energy in order to dig up wisdom—it does not come knocking at our door. THREE: A prevailing cultural attitude states "wisdom is not that important." After a careful review of the preceding three observations, we begin to make sense of one of the statements spoken by Jesus: narrow is the way and few there be that find it.

> ...the only way in which a human being can make some approach to knowing the whole of a subject, is by hearing what can be said about it by persons of every variety of opinion, and studying all modes in which it can be looked at by every character of mind. No wise man ever acquired his wisdom in any mode but this; nor is it in the nature of human intellect to become wise in any other manner. **J.S. MILL 13**

REFERENCES

1. Plato. *Great books of the western world*. (Hereinafter referred to by volume number only). 1982 edition, twenty-fourth printing. Chicago: Encyclopaedia Britannica. Volume 7. Page 8.

2. Hazlitt, Frances and Henry (1984). *The wisdom of the stoics.* Lanham, New York and London: University Press of America. Page 47.

3. Super, Charles William (1902). *Wisdom and will in education.* Harrisburg, PA: R.L. Myers. Page 52.

4. Epictetus. Volume 12. Page 135.

5. *The Holy Bible.* London: Oxford University Press.

6. Plotinus. Volume 17. Page 92.

7. Plato. Volume 7. Page 228.

8. Bacon, Francis. Volume 30. Page 121.

9. Plotinus. Volume 17. Page 90.

10. Nietzsche (1965). *Schopenhauer as educator.* Chicago: Regenery. Page 54.

11. Tacitus. Volume 15. Page 23.

12. Lawson, D.E. (1961). *Wisdom and education.* Carbondale: Southern Illinois University Press. Page vii.

13. Mill, J.S. Volume 43. Page 276.

CHAPTER TWO

DEVELOPMENT vs. SELF-DESTRUCTION

D evelopment is a process which continues expanding to higher levels whereas self-destruction consistently moves in the reverse direction. By development, we are not referring to an increase of industrial output; we mean an increase of natural abilities—caring, loving, thinking, emotional maturity and the development of talents, particularly talents which are unrelated to office, attention from others, money and prestige. How many so-called successful individuals can honestly assert that "time" is their friend in the expansion of their natural abilities and virtues with each passing year? "Time" is the enemy for an increasing number of people and each passing year gives evidence of the dwindling of courage, rational thoughts and understanding.

Human beings may avail themselves of many avenues of development: emotional, spiritual, intellectual, social, physical and intuitive. Each avenue contributes to the ever-renewing creation of a self-actualized person. Failure to develop one or more dimensions limits the potential of other dimensions. A holistic individual strives to integrate many areas of development and "time" is highly cherished.

Eighty years pass like lightning for the developing person and can pass as quickly for a non-developing individual (for example, one habituated to the stupor resulting from drug and alcohol abuse). But ... the end of both lives provides evidence of a major difference. One peacefully accepts death (after developing genuine experience of life's offering). The other (agitated by daze and distraction) has little to die for.

The Law of Development finds support in the Parable of the Talents:

> For to every one who has shall more be given, and he shall have an abundance [development]; but from the one who does not have, even what he does have shall be taken away [failure to develop].   **(Matthew 25:29)** 1

The second part of the parable is written in mystifying language: how is it possible to take away "from the one who does not have?" Developmental potential is inherent within everyone. There are time limitations during which certain stages of growth flourish; failure of a minimal response to develop results in the near impossibility of development later on (even the potential is taken away). Jesus added in the following verse: "And cast out the worthless slave into outer darkness..." This sounds like Darwin's "survival of the fittest." A full understanding of Darwin's "survival of the fittest" recognizes the following point:

> In vain did some naturalists point out that success in the struggle for existence is at least as often achieved among animals by co-operation and mutual help as by competition and combat.   **DOBZHANSKY** 2

Failure to understand that "cooperation and mutual help" translate into mutual benefit, subtracts from the meaning of the preceding quote.

> Developmental arrest begins in our infancy. I use the term kronist to designate parents who devour their children psychologically. There are various ways of doing this. Among civilized people, favored ploys are prolonging their infancy, transforming them into psychologically dependent creatures, stifling their self-reliance, and preventing them from developing in accordance with their innate potentialities and desires. The kronist often is, or appears to be, devoted to the children he suffocates.   **N. WEYL** 3

Trauma is not easy to overcome, so it is understandable that we cling to whatever is available to sooth our wounds. Children who are psychologically devoured can not avoid trauma. Later in life we consume large quantities of alcohol, food and drugs—habits which interfere with our authentic participation in life by the substitution of relentless pursuit of distraction. Neither consumption nor distraction frees us from the paralysis of trauma. "I feel better" leads to habit. Energy robbing habits stand in the way of self-actualization.

> ...pleasure, to deceive us, marches before and conceals
> her train.   **MONTAIGNE 4**

A good feeling today can lead to a raunchy feeling tomorrow. The soothing substance which results in a vice has similar value to strong medication for the mentally ill. Both buy time; neither permanently alters the source of trouble.

We can be enslaved to money, power, sex, alcohol, drugs, food, nicotine, glamour, wishful religious thinking, ourselves (narcissism) and mindlessness. Slavery is the incontestable enemy of freedom. Voluntary, sustained freedom of choice works against slavery. Involuntary enslavement to any vice negates freedom of choice.

Self-destruction occurs on the basis of non-use (neglect) and abuse (misuse of developmental potential). Neglect is instanced in the failure to develop.

Every child is presented with thoughts on good and evil. We were told to seek and partake of goodness.

> It is only man who is good, and he is good only because
> he can also be evil.   **HEGEL 5**

The term "good" is often associated with good behavior. This view of "good" can be misleading. A good boy or a good girl are so-called based upon their willingness to conform. Strangely enough, conformity can work against development. A developing individual is able to conform and in addition, recognizes when conformity is self-limiting. Conformity in and of itself provides little information; how and what we conform to is meaningful.

Either our thoughts and actions are moving in the direction of good or they are moving in the direction of evil. This developmental standard removes the slop and slack of unseasoned thinking. Just as time does not stand still, (time plucks "the keen teeth from the fierce tiger's jaws"—regrettably, I do not remember the poet who wrote this), development requires continual movement. The most significant Law of Development: by virtue of not going forward we go backward.

> The unconscious is pure nature, and, like nature, pours out its gifts in profusion. But left to itself and without the human response from consciousness, it can (again like nature) destroy its own gifts and sooner or later sweep them into annihilation. **C.J. JUNG 6**

Human beings are not designed like some machines which can be stored for a length of time and when reactivated, function as before.

Admittedly, I place extraordinary emphasis on development. Until 1900, development for a majority of citizens was not as crucial as it is today. Jets and rockets, satellites and lasers, population explosion and unlimited greed, computers and robots—all of these have completely altered the context of the world.

We must accept and incorporate technological advances, but equally, if not more important, the evolution of mental capacity is vital if we are to reduce the present cold-hearted inhumanity. Whether we examine the Roman Empire or present-day America, when considering decadence as reflected in lust, luxury and cruelty, the perverseness of evil is not a return to a lower estate (beasts), but the corruption of a higher one. Modern man does not regress to the state of "primitive;" he does worse by presenting ample evidence for an increase of vicious brutality. Unlimited opportunity for vice combined with the increasing availability of money, call for even stronger character than was necessary one hundred years ago. Never before has there been a quantum leap in the number of people who are able to spend time and money haphazardly, particularly when viewed from the angle of endless opportunities provided by technological progress.

> Many were in love with triflers like themselves, and many fancied that they were in love when in truth they were only idle. Their affection was seldom fixed on sense or virtue, and therefore seldom ended but in vexation. **S. JOHNSON 7**

It is important to recognize that a country with the greatest technological development is very vulnerable when there are low standards or an absence of standards. A country is no stronger than the combined strength of its citizens. What is the value of a technologically advanced country which degenerates for the very reason that people lack reverence for matters pertaining to living life well? This refers to millions of people who fail to develop convictions based on principle, who justify cultural degeneracy by claiming—"isn't everybody doing it"—and finally, those who sincerely believe that money and material comfort are the only issues worthy of discussion and pursuit.

Weakness of character proves to be the greatest weapon. Ironically, this kind of demise is self-inflicted. Low cultural standards in a technologically advanced country are like a malignant cancer which destroys the body. Both are eaten alive from within. In the end neither technological superiority nor advanced medical assistance can restore the former quality of life.

Returning to good and evil:

> But the individual is evil only when the natural manifests itself in mere sensual desire—when an unrighteous will presents itself in its untamed, untrained, violent shape... **HEGEL 8**

There are two key words in the preceding quote: "only" and "mere." Sensual desire which exclusively maintains itself in untamed, untrained and violent shape, is evil. Development is the counterpoise to an untamed, untrained and violent condition. The "natural" offers far greater possibilities than mere sensual desire.

Human beings are designed to be more than animals; the faculty of thinking distinguishes us from brutes (assuming that we develop rational minds). Our senses are designed to enhance mental development; by all means the purpose of our senses is not to obstruct mental development. Our sense-experience and neurological system combine in forming a cumulative record of the life we live. The nervous system is miraculously intertwined with the mind. To the extent we irremediably destroy our nervous system, we reduce the usefulness of our minds.

We also know there is a genetic factor of neurological function. The nerves do not tell a lie, particularly when they are abused. To the extent we develop our minds, we differ from the brutes; to the extent we live only in the senses, we become far worse than brutes. Each of us is confronted daily with the challenge of examining sense-experience; specifically, the direction in which our sense-experience takes us. The oft-repeated comment of Socrates comes to mind: a life unexamined is not worth living.

How can we know when our senses are enlivening and enculturating our minds?

> ...refined pleasures and enjoyments...do not wear out,
> but rather increase the capacity for further enjoyment
> of them, and while they delight they at the same time
> cultivate.   KANT 9

True enjoyment and lasting happiness are possible insofar as our experience with pleasure cultivates us. There is an important distinction between happiness and pleasure. Pleasure is sensory pleasure; happiness is long-term pleasure. For example, a person goes to the dentist and is happy to get his or her teeth fixed, but this is not pleasure.

Championing mental development is not a popular theme. A case in point is my brother's only question about this book—how will it make him richer? There is a similarity of mentality between one who lives solely for sensual experience and one who entirely pursues wealth.

> A man immersed in life who can see nothing save the
> interests of the world, of power, of money, and position
> and rivalry, is dead. In the same way men are divided
> into those who are asleep and those awake.
>   M. NICOLL 10

Power, money and position should not be the end goal, but rather means to other ends, e.g., to develop our minds, to strengthen our character and to advance culture.

Involvement with evil does one of two things: 1) promotes more evil, or 2) after being repulsed by evil, sends us in the direction of good. Sometimes a good person is viewed as a dull and limited individual. This is especially true when an individual who is perceived as "good" fails to develop. Development is not a one-way ticket to confinement; it is an opportunity for unhampered exploration and positive accomplishment.

Just as an individual fails to develop, an entire nation can abort development. Expansion is not proof of development; it is simply evidence of quantitative change. Minimally, development requires qualitative change; occasionally it includes quantitative change. A case in point illustrates quantitative change absent development:

> ...objects acquired for the purpose of countering boredom

reveal in rather short order their inability to do so in any durable fashion, yet continue to "hang around," they themselves come to exude the boredom they have been unable to conquer.   **A.O. HIRSCHMAN** 11

Persistent boredom makes evident the lack of quality in our lives. Obtaining more material goods (often, none other than a quantitative change) in hope of combating boredom only purchases distraction time. Distractions at best provide limited relief; sooner or later we return to the wasteland of our lives. Material goods which facilitate development do not bore us.

Mankind therefore ever toils vainly and to no purpose and wastes life in groundless cares, because sure enough they have not learnt what is the true end of getting and up to what point genuine pleasure goes on increasing...
     LUCRETIUS 12

Pleasure which burns itself out is quantitative pleasure, whereas pleasure which contributes to development is qualitative pleasure. The aim of this commentary on pleasure is not to deprive or reduce pleasure. We have the obligation to take a serious look at our experience of pleasure and discover the role it plays in our lives. Qualitative pleasure (which continues to increase) is admirable. Frivolous pleasure which robs us of future possibilities of pleasure is despicable and ought to be avoided. Our desire, focus and experience of pleasure require intelligent observation and understanding.

I estimate that less than twenty percent of the population suffer from a lack of pleasure. Other individuals (over fifty percent) seek pleasure as an end in itself. This relationship with pleasure leads neither to lasting satisfaction nor to serenity. A case in point is the stimulation of our taste buds with a steady diet of junk food, which despite its pleasing taste is eventually detrimental to our health and physical appearance. Nutritious food, on the other hand, develops and maintains bodily health. In the same way, our experience with pleasure either cultivates us and lasts through the years or results in premature and excessive deterioration.

Actually, the substitution of the reality-principle for the pleasure-principle denotes no dethronement of the pleasure-principle, but only a safeguarding of it. A momentary pleasure, uncertain in its results is given up, but

> only in order to gain in the new way an assured pleasure
> coming later.   **FREUD 13**

The endless ways people foolishly spend money and waste time is self-defeating. In visiting the nations of this world (particularly those where vast sums of money and goods exchange hands), we can not help but think: human beings exist for the purpose of playing and the earth is their playground. When generation after generation trade their greatest opportunity (mental development) for distractions culminating in an empty-headed passing of time, that nation can not remain strong for long.

Mental development is not assured on the basis of a successful job or an increase of knowledge. Sometimes a prestigious job results in one being worse off rather than improved thereby. For example, without strength of character, earning lots of money can speed up the process of degeneration more than would be the case otherwise. Large sums of money provide greater means with which to dismantle our bodies and minds. Admittedly, this is not a pleasant or readily received topic. Nonetheless, let every citizen who proclaims, "I love America," recognize the urgency of forethought and swift action in providing substance and meaning for loving America. Complacency will not survive in a competitive world. With expanding populations and the evolution of higher standards in several leading countries, competition determines who and what survives.

> Undoubtedly one of the most urgent tasks of a science of ethics at the present juncture is to analyze and separate the role of true compassion from that of mutual indulgence, Hedonism, and the rejection of any painfully exacting standards.   **R.B. CATTELL 14**

True compassion is distinguished from weak sentimentality on the basis of development. Compassion should strengthen rather than weaken the receiver. Forgiveness evolves out of compassion. The goal of forgiving is not license to repeat errors. To forgive is to inspire improvement in the one forgiven. "Compassion" which results in a continuation of foolishness is not compassion. True compassion reduces the need for compassion. There are great tragedies which call for unlimited compassion; these situations are evident. Forgiveness and compassion which increase helplessness lead to a vicious cycle of falsehood. If dignity and self-esteem are not forthcoming for the recipient of compassion, then the energy of "compassion" in this instance is not worthy of mention.

What do we conclude about development?

1) Failure to develop limits the opportunity to develop.
2) Standards promote development.
3) Due to a technological revolution, the development of humanity is more urgent today than ever before.
4) Development can be recognized on the basis of positive change.
5) Meaningful development requires qualitative change.
6) Substitution of the reality-principle for the pleasure-principle furthers development.
7) Forgiveness and compassion are of value to the extent they result in inspiration which leads to development.

Our civilization is at a crossroad with respect to sexual development. We have always proclaimed the right to privacy and the right to our particular brand of happiness. Beginning in the 1960's, we claim the right to unrestricted sexual experience. Thoughts pertaining to rights are one matter; indisputably, the dictates of nature hold the greater potency.

> Freud once made the ironic observation that modern sex impresses him as representing a dying function. This joke may, for all we know, contain more truth than one would generally credit to a casual remark.
> **E. BERGLER 15**

What do we want from our sexual experiences? What thoughts are coursing through our minds when we seek to engage sexually? First and foremost, ideal sexual experience pursues development along emotional, psychological, intellectual and spiritual lines. There is also the benefit of physical development. Sexual experience exclusively focused on sensual pleasure shows disregard for emotional and mental development.

Where do we begin to reform the chaos of sexual attitudes, beliefs and practices? The golden calf as a god of sex must be dethroned in our culture. America displays sexual immaturity by shifting from one extreme to another in regard to the cultural emphasis on sexuality. One century ago the cultural standard pretended that human sexuality was virtually nonexistent. Today our culture proclaims that life is sexuality: without direct and subtle sexual emphasis, there is no life. A visitor from another planet could not help but think that were it not for the present multi-billion dollar ad campaign (whose primary aim relentlessly exploits sex), everyone would lose interest in all things sexual in one night. Or has life become so futile and boring that nothing short of a sexual theme can hold our attention for more than five minutes?

The integrity of every human being is strongly related to the experience of his or her sexual history. The dependence on good looks, money, alcohol, power, office, lying and all other modes of mutual deception (in order to increase the chances of going to bed with somebody), reveal a total disregard for integrity. Both sexes use base tactics and motives for cajoling one another into bed, resulting all too frequently in unsatisfactory sexual experiences. We can not begin with dishonesty and end in fulfillment.

Insecurity ranks high in its contribution to unsuccessful relationships. Whether in or out of a relationship, we nonetheless appear to be insecure. Without a platform of honest sharing and values worthy of mutual support, it is difficult to feel secure in a relationship.

During the 1960's and 1970's, androgyny was extolled in American colleges and universities. Males were encouraged to develop their feminine side and females were encouraged to develop their masculine side. What the extollers left out is the fact that a male does not qualify for being androgynous by developing his feminine side at the expense of failing to develop his masculinity; and, neither does a female qualify for being androgynous by developing her masculine side at the expense of failing to develop her femininity.

Life was designed to be lived and a progressive lifestyle can be recommended to future generations. Perhaps we ought to begin asking ourselves whether our thinking and behavior are what we would admire in our children. We can not afford to be naive.

Self-destruction follows on the heels of a sadistic appetite which seeks to destroy others. After long consideration, we have no alternative but to say "yes" in responding to Samuel Johnson's question:

> Is there such depravity in man, as that he should injure another without benefit to himself? **S. JOHNSON 16**

This chapter makes an urgent appeal for development. Furthermore, failure to develop in today's world guarantees destruction from within and from without. Development requires an admirable destiny. Two centuries ago, Hegel accurately identified the destiny of development:

> The highest point in the development of a people is this—to have gained a conception of its life and condition, to have reduced its laws, its ideas of justice and morality to a science; for in this unity lies the most intimate unity that spirit can attain to in and with itself.
>
> **HEGEL 17**

REFERENCES

1. *The Holy Bible.* London: Oxford University Press.

2. Dobzhansky. (1964). *Heredity and the nature of man.* New York and Toronto: The New American Library. Page 153.

3. Weyl, N. (1980). *Karl Marx: Racist.* New Rochelle, NY: Arlington House. Page 255.

4. Montaigne. Volume 25. Page 111.

5. Hegel. Volume 46. Page 130.

6. Jung, C. (1964). *Man and his symbols.* Garden City, NY: Doubleday. Page 258.

7. Johnson, S. (1976). *The history of Rasselas, prince of abissinia*. New York: Penguin Books. Page 91.

8. Hegel. Volume 46. Page 354.

9. Kant. Volume 42. Page 299.

10. Nicoll, M. (1950). *The new man*. London: Vincent Stuart. Page 107.

11. Hirschmann, A.O. (1982). *Shifting involvements; private interest and public action*. Princeton, NJ: Princeton University Press. Page 57.

12. Lucretius. Volume 12. Page 79.

13. Freud, S. (1959). *Collected papers*. New York: Basic Books. Volume IV, Page 18.

14.` Cattell, R.B. (1972). *A new morality from science: Beyondism*. New York: Pergamon. Page 453.

15. Bergler, E. (1961). *Counterfeit-sex: homosexuality, impotence, frigidity*. New York: Grove Press. Page 369.

16. Johnson, S. (1976). *The history of Rasselas, prince of abissinia*. New York: Penguin Books. Page 58.

17. Hegel. Volume 46. Page 188.

CHAPTER THREE

TOWARD AN OPEN MIND

A n untoward disease, that a man should be so riveted to his own belief as to fancy that others cannot believe otherwise than as he does...   **MONTAIGNE 1**

Belief and conviction are necessary; the larger question concerns itself with <u>how</u> we arrive at belief and conviction. Reception to new ideas combined with depth of conviction challenge our thinking. Belief systems which fear open challenge have something to hide. Institutions which demand blind devotion seek to maintain an arrangement by which to take advantage of the laws of the land, of the ignorance of people, their ineptitude and false worship. Many interpret and experience blind devotion as security. We are "secure" until courageous individuals point out glaring abuses.

When we release the stranglehold of our beliefs (in order to view contrary and alternate perspectives), we experience fear of the unknown. Resistance to insight, present in a rigid system of beliefs, constitutes evidence of falsehood. We fear insight because awareness of truth requires change. We prefer to avoid change and continue the practice of living a lie.

Preoccupation in our faith reveals uncertainty of proclaimed believing. We are preoccupied with a belief because we are unsure of what it is we believe. The less secure we are in our faith, the greater our need for others to "believe" as we "believe."

...preoccupied by the impress of something else, we are
withheld under that pressure from becoming aware of
The Unity; a mind gripped and fastened by some definite
thing cannot take the print of the very contrary.

PLOTINUS 2

Some impose upon the world that they believe that
which they do not believe; others, more in number, make
themselves believe that they believe, not being able to
penetrate into what it is to believe...   MONTAIGNE 3

Adequate inquiry into the development and acquisition of
beliefs frees us from the urge to impose thoughts on others. It
takes years to develop a foundation secure enough to withstand
earthquakes of confusion and deception. Many individuals have
a platform whereby they seek to acquire admirers and followers.
Almost no one offers to take responsibility when the platform
crashes twenty years hence, if not tomorrow. It is supported by
pillars made of plaster of paris rather than pillars of marble. A
coat of highly advanced painting technique disguises the plaster
of paris as marble.   Only the rarest individual discerns the
difference.

We have freedom of speech and we voice millions of ideas
(opinions), most of which will not hold up in time, even though the
sound of them has a pleasing ring. The freedom and ability to
think clearly contributes more to civilization than mere freedom
of speech. Unintelligible and incomplete speech (disguised as
"freedom") prevent clear thinking. We must recognize the difference between Freedom of Speech and Freedom to Speak Intelli-
gibly.

To have or not to have freedom of speech is not a question to
be debated; the issue at hand recognizes freedom of speech as
having either a positive or negative effect upon the ethics and
morals of society.   Freedom without personal responsibility
undermines civilization. The challenge for every citizen is to
explore and discover which ideas have the substance of marble
and which ones disintegrate (like the plaster of paris), after
several rain storms.

The result of extended inquiry yields an opportunity to
perceive relationships (when and how two items or qualities go
together); this braces us with the courage to face the unknown.

...by genius I mean those people who have really outstanding ability to see the relatedness of events, which

seems to be the ultimate of the measurable intelligence
factors.   H.S. SULLLIVAN 4

Rugged individuals grounded in the wisdom of the ancients maintain open minds. An open mind is not a mind open to an unending stream of idiotic, contradictory, self-destructive and unethical thoughts spewing forth daily from the marketplace. In giving full attention to a barrage of retrograde and unreflecting ideas, little time remains for inspiring, moral, cultivated and refined thoughts.

The development of the mind is through perceiving finer
and finer meanings. It develops by becoming aware of
finer and finer distinctions.   M. NICOLL 5

This requires time, and time well spent is not a national favorite. We prefer to engage in that which gives immediate gratification. Many find it difficult to dig to bedrock and probe the depth of their beliefs and convictions.

Who needs to be aware of the conditions for developing an open mind? Every human being. Some individuals believe they possess an open mind claiming that liberal-minded parents provided an environment whereby they could entertain whatever thoughts they chose. An open mind is not at the mercy of an unrestrained flood of indulgent notions. What kind of life would it be to weigh thousands of strange ideas which issue forth every day? We could waste a lifetime wading through nonsense and never harvest due to an excess of an important substance— fertilizer.

An open mind has a history of reading worthwhile material, of evincing personal honesty, and of conversing with exceptional individuals. It does not seek material comfort as the number one motivating factor in life. An open mind develops an inner quietude which takes advantage of feedback by being able to hear our thoughts. With the help of intuition, we are able to recognize the merit and demerit of passing ideas—from a distance. Everybody wants an open mind; few there be who are willing to invest the energy and integrity to acquire it. The fine art of maintaining an open mind works against rubbish, which jeopardizes the faculty of clear thinking.

...it is exactly people's feeling of being righteous, of being
in the right, that prevents them from changing. They
are not satisfied with themselves. It is only others who

> are wrong, not themselves. And it is their feeling of being already righteous and in the right that determines their special forms of justifying themselves. From this they derive their feeling of worth and merit, and it is just here that they are most easily upset, most easily offended. Is anything more easy than being offended and giving offence? This is the human situation. The extraordinarily harsh teaching of the Gospels is to break this feeling of merit and complacency that everyone openly or secretly rests upon, and this is the source of being offended.   **M. NICOLL 6**

"Special forms of justifying themselves" are beliefs. There are no limits to the arrangement of beliefs human beings conjure up. Belief is all too often a handy compromise which initially falls on the personally "advantageous" side. Some change their beliefs as often as necessary (without paying attention to principle), to match their goal. Others never alter their beliefs for fear of the unknown. Belief in and of itself is insufficient; conviction based upon principle is far more stable. Belief is often self-justification and convenient rationalization.

An open mind does not resist challenges to cherished beliefs. This is a matter of personal honesty and integrity. Truth defends itself. When we are uncomfortable and threatened by different and inscrutable ideas, we reveal uncertainty of thoughts we claim to hold dear. Stability, security and growth are the result of sound thinking.

Recently, the institution of marriage has come under attack. One-half of all marriages end in divorce and frequently, one or both parties marry for reasons which get in the way of loving one another. Marriage ought not be downgraded on the basis of a presently faltering track record and a multitude marrying for reasons which are incompatible with success in marriage. It is much easier to blame the institution of marriage rather than take a hard look at our own motives for actions (which requires an open and courageous mind).

The success or failure of marriage depends in great part on the will, honesty and character of those who marry. No one said it would be easy. We should not expect success when we begin in falsehood. We respect honesty, progress and success in marriage. Successful marriage requires outstanding courage and integrity in the modern and complex world.

An open mind learns to take total responsibility for choices and outcomes in life. To the degree we choose to ignore responsibility, our minds are closed.

A major obstacle for developing an open mind resides in the overpowering habit of manipulating others. Having to control others betrays a severe lack of self-control. An insecure, frightened and demanding individual presumes it necessary to control others. By jumping the gun and disallowing others to choose, the avenue to natural and unpretentious feedback from others is blocked. People respond differently when they are threatened. Those who abuse power will one day find themselves at the mercy of power.

Maturity favors an open mind. The more senseless the prevalent and floating ideas of a culture, the greater the challenge for developing and maintaining an open mind. It means our discriminating ability must be very strong in order to separate wheat from chaff.

How is keen discrimination developed? By seeking out and respecting others who are brighter, more honest, caring and aware, and have acquired emotional stability. This endeavor continues without end if we esteem the possession of an open mind.

> ...the worst and most rancorous kind of envy, the envy of superiority of understanding. **H. FIELDING** 7

Frequently belief is a cover for ignorance. Fear of the unknown promotes limited, rigid beliefs. There are ample ready-made beliefs on every street corner. People have many beliefs from which they love to be unburdened. If we listen to bystanders, they fill our ears and make no apology in the event we become equally confused. Do not make the mistake of assuming that the speaker accepts responsibility if the idea fails to work, misleads or backfires. Without inquiry, prior to adopting beliefs, assumption is like walking on the quicksand of a mental swampland. Mature belief is recognized in its promotion of inquiry whereas ungrounded belief is threatened by inquiry.

> Study and inquiry alone can provide that liberality of judgment without which it is impossible to acquire new knowledge or even to preserve what we have. For we submit to certain received ideas not because they are true but because they are powerful.
> **MADAME DE STAEL** 8

How do we know what to study? Which questions are pertinent? Printing presses disseminate information at an unprecedented rate. When issues arise, the media provide a standard set of questions and answers. These questions often evade the central issue and give an appearance of adequate investigation.

Study is vital for developing an open mind, but, it must be well-focused study of books with solid content. Certainly the classics are for the most part foolproof. We must be patient since it requires a major investment of interest and stamina to read the classics. At the same time, there is no greater return per hour invested. The classics provide a return which continues to reward throughout the days of our lives.

The experience of developing an open, honest and unadulterated mind is one of the greatest treasures in life. It is next to impossible to close what took hard work and years to open. Assent to the value of an open mind is quickly forthcoming, yet . . . intuition tells us that only a small number of individuals are willing to invest the time and thinking essential for acquiring an open mind.

> Then to from small indications we draw the widest inferences and by our own fault entangle ourselves in the meshes of self-delusion.   **LUCRETIUS 9**

A particular frame of mind facilitates the development of an open mind:

> We must be humble and put sympathies and antipathies honourably in the background if we would learn to know reality in this world.   **FREUD 10**

Conversely, the following frame of mind works against development of an open mind.

> I mean the narrow-mindedness shown by the best intellects, their inaccessibility to the most forcible arguments, their uncritical credulity for the most disputable assertions.   **FREUD 11**

Certainly in religious matters lies "uncritical credulity for the most disputable assertions." Everyone has the the need to believe something. It is not our intention to rob anyone of personally cherished beliefs. The aim of this chapter is a request for everyone to investigate what it is they believe, and whether it is wise to continue with <u>all</u> of the beliefs we have become accustomed to believe.

> Be large-minded enough to believe, that men may rea-
> son and feel very differently from yourselves: how is it
> that men, when left to themselves, fall into such various
> forms of religion, except that there are various types of
> mind among them, very distinct from each other?
> **J.H. NEWMAN 12**

Look around and behold the world we have created. Think hard and remember what has gone before us in past centuries. Now is a very special moment in the life of humankind: we are faced with an awesome choice which will result in two completely different outcomes:

1) a return to barbarism which will be called, The New Dark Age, or
2) unrivaled progress in human cooperation and competition (between individuals and nation to nation), which of and by itself will vastly improve the quality of life for a majority of citizens around the world, whether poor or rich, black or white. The next leap forward begins with honest and dedicated people who revere life by seizing the moment and develop intolerance for injustice, lying and evil.

> In the main the question is how light or how heavy we
> are—the problem of our 'specific gravity'. One has to be
> very light to drive one's will to knowledge into such a dis-
> tance and, as it were, beyond one's time, to create for one-
> self eyes to survey millenia and, moreover, clear skies in
> those eyes. **NIETZSCHE 13**

REFERENCES

1. Montaigne. Volume 25. Page 153.

2. Plotinus. Volume 17. Page 358.

3. Montaigne. Volume 25. Page 210.

4. Sullivan, H.S. (1953). *The interpersonal theory of psychiatry.* New York: Norton. Page 23.

5. Nicoll, M. (1950). *The new man.* London: Vincent Stuart. Page 138.

6. Ibid. Page 62.

7. Fielding. Volume 37. Page 235.

8. de Stael, Madame (1964). *On politics, literature and national character.* Garden City, New York: Doubleday. Page 277.

9. Lucretius. Volume 12. Page 54.

10. Freud, S. (1920, 1935). *A general introduction to psychoanalysis.* Tr. Joan Riviere. NY: Liveright. Page 130.

11. Freud, S. (1959). *Collected papers.* New York: Basic Books. Volume IV, Page 302.

12. Newman, J.H. (1968). *Apologia pro vita sua.* New York: W.W. Norton. Edited by David J. DeLaura. Page 195.

13. Schacht, R. (1983). *Nietzsche.* London: Routledge & Kegan Paul. Page 44.

CHAPTER FOUR

KNOWLEDGE vs. IGNORANCE

Often it is said, "ignorance is bliss." In hearkening back to days of innocence, how far have we strayed? Blissful ignorance is no longer a viable option. The game plan has changed. Acceleration of the challenge to survive requires the discovery and employment of useful knowledge. It is better to know little with some ability for conceptualization than to know a lot with limited ability to conceptualize.

This chapter presents the interdependence of two kinds of knowledge: technology and the knowledge of relationships among human beings.

The arms race has been in full force for more than four decades. Simultaneously, another race has been in progress for nearly two centuries: the race between human development and technology. Discouragingly, as technology has advanced, practical ethics have stood still.

Idealistic thinking presumes that science will solve our human neglect. Human neglect is observed in the lack of progress in human relations (individual to individual and nation to nation), in view of the benefits of technological progress. Take the medium of television—certainly a technological breakthrough. Most people perceive television primarily as a medium of entertainment. Television has the potential of raising our cultural standard by increasing people's mental development. Instead, the overall effect tends to reduce mental effectiveness. As long as we provide unlimited numbers of solely entertaining programs (the kind which induce mesmerization), unlimited numbers of people will continue to choose these over and above public television and other worthwhile programs. Admittedly, the average television show reflects our cultural taste, which tends more toward mediocrity than excellence.

An increase in technology has strained the human factor to the breaking point. Now we are inescapably one global family. Jet transportation, satellite communications, technology exchange and theft, cultural adoption and English as a universal language have brought us together. The population explosion adds more stress.

> Competition will never cease. This is a piece of knowledge that many wish not to think about. In spite of its historical stress, a permanent need for accepting competition and developing rules of the game are the price we pay for evolution. Under stress people want to ignore this piece of knowledge
> **(RAYMOND B. CATTELL,** *Personal Communication).*

Historically, when a nation engaged in war, it fought until it conquered or was vanquished. The greatest exception is Japan which surrendered at the end of World War II without being exploited by the victors. MacArthur established guidelines for the operation of Japanese government following the war. Japan was coerced to make several concessions, many of which have been favorable (for example, Shinto priests were removed from the payroll of the government). Even though millions of dollars of aid were given to West Germany, the situation is different for Germany which was divided into East Germany and West Germany.

Mutually assured destruction greatly restricts and possibly eliminates belligerence on a large scale against another country anywhere in the world. For the first time victory could also mean annihilation. The prospect of nuclear war forces nations to cooperate militarily. How effectively are today's nations collaborating? Rather than fair play, cutthroat competition does not cease.

> This refers in particular to economic and cultural competition. We will always be an endangered species of cul-

ture— this is a piece of knowledge one has to accept
(RAYMOND B. CATTELL, *Personal Communication*).

Economic war is substituted for military war. Victory belongs to the nation or nations of economic superiority. Competition should be put on a new level. That level would promote competition for Nobel prizes, competition for cultural achievements, productivity and especially competition for scientific contributions which add quality to the life experience of the citizens of all nations.

> We must view with profound respect the infinite capacity of the human mind to resist the introduction of useful knowledge. **T.R. LOUNSBURY** 1

If this is true, then we know that the promotion of useful knowledge requires persistent effort. Tomes upon tomes of research collect every year, more so with the advent of computer research. Much of the research is simply an exercise in research and yields little useful knowledge. Yet we must not discontinue research. Rather we must raise the level of research thinking.

> ...the ignorant man has no conception of his ignorance, because he has no conception of knowledge. **KANT 2**

"Research" is high sounding. Considering the proliferation of research in general, recent advances in the field of human relationships are insignificant.

Whatever age we may be, let us pause and look into our minds. What do we find and how did it get there? From the time of birth, we have heard thousands of ideas some of which we adopted, unaware of whether they were true or false. Our adoptions resemble the limitations of our ability to think. Before long, boundaries of thinking patterns are established. These are referred to as personal thought parameter (PTP). Beyond the age of twenty, only one in a thousand experiences a noticeable expansion of personal thought parameter (PTP).

> The average person stopping at twenty is due to failure of personal individual thought to lead to anything but inconsistencies. People give up. They say there are some things we can't reason out. Take the question of restraint on sexuality. One group says, "We can't see any sense in restraint." Another group says, "restraint is

necessary because of the romantic conflicts which arise"
(**RAYMOND B. CATTELL**, *Personal Communication*).

Without seasoned and progressive input into our minds, nothing changes. Habit can be positive (discipline, character, generosity, honesty, etc.); certainly habit is often negative (alcohol and drug abuse, selecting television programs which reinforce passivity of mind, disregard for others and self-deception). When applied to patterns of thinking, routine prematurely and indiscriminately locks in our PTP according to the limitations of our exposure. For example, in reading a book, most of the time we only absorb that which concurs with our pre-established thinking. Our thoughts rarely exceed the restrictions of habitual modes of thinking. In addition, the people we associate with (and their level of mental development) play a significant role in the thoughts we embrace and the identity we assume.

Look at this from group phenomenon. Every idea has a certain percolation range which can be defined in terms of IQ. The idea that free trade is more beneficial than protectionism is understood before it can be adopted. Other examples are Galileo and Copernicus: after all, there are still about five percent of people who believe the earth is flat. It has taken four centuries for Galileo's notion that the earth moves, to affect the thinking for ninety-five percent of the population
(**RAYMOND B. CATTELL**, *Personal Communication*).

We are exhorted to have an open mind which expands our PTP. Flexibility permits retreat. By retreat, we mean doubting established truths. Untutored minds are inflexible minds.

Few men can think long without running into a confusion of ideas, and mistaking one for another; and there are various degrees of this infirmity.   **DAVID HUME 3**

For, let us make no mistake, it is biological evolution of mental capacity, and not merely an accumulation of scientific research data that is needed.
R.B. CATTELL 4

An uninspired mind does not innovate. Knowledge alone does not inspire. Even worse, information frequently passes for knowledge. An information explosion bombards our eardrums, the value of which is questionable. Could a barrage of information keep us from discovering useful knowledge, or at least from integrating some of the knowledge we have become aware of? For example, there is a tremendous knowledge of nutrition and fitness; however, we also have an excess of malnutrition, overweight and a lack of physical fitness. The knowledge we possess commonly falls short of translating into benefit. Our vulnerability to faulty appetite and laziness (in spite of known hazards) is the result of turning a deaf ear to the facts of nutrition and fitness. The lack of proper exercise and malnutrition (due to overeating junk foods), undermine mental strength. This illustration shows how knowledge and ignorance can go hand in hand.

The law of mental parameter states: stop expanding mentally and our PTP locks into position. Somewhere between the boundless curiosity of a six year old child and the inconsequential views and limited conclusions of a twenty year old (or any age thereafter), our minds turn off. One might object by citing the millions of college students, graduates and Ph.D. candidates and surely their capacity to generate thinking has not closed down. At the present time, the majority of the aforementioned fail to generate serious independent thinking. The major requirements for academic "success" today are ears readily capable of listening, memory function, imitation and a willingness to suffer boredom (a symptom which reveals a lack of whole-hearted and honest participation). To "succeed" in higher education requires faking ability and denial of personal experience. The preceding statement sounds facetious but may contain more truth than falsehood. Our present educational system, to a significant degree, does not provoke learning; it encourages mediocrity. Those who have learned the art of regurgitation experience the least trauma and receive excellent marks. Unfortunately, as the ability to regurgitate increases, the ability to think independently decreases.

> ...an unreasoning life; such a life is too feeble in being; it is reason dissipated, it is indetermination; only in the measure of approach towards reason is there liberation from happening; the rational is above chance...the root of reason is self-springing.   **PLOTINUS 5**

Historically, reason was unalloyed with manipulation and excuse. "Reason" no longer holds a respectable position having been watered down and associated with the common winds of opinion.

Reason cannot trouble herself with opinions.   **KANT 6**

Democracy gives everyone an opportunity to voice his/her opinion. Of what value are nonsensical opinions when they cloud real issues and hinder the attainment of a well-reasoned critical edge? By the time we listen to a medley of unsupportable ideas, the silly conclusions we draw and inept laws we pass are to be expected. This will not change until we raise our standard of thinking. For example, our congressional leaders are not worthy of imitation or envy.

> ...ignorance itself, without malice, is able to make a man both to believe lies and tell them, and sometimes also to invent them.   **THOMAS HOBBES 7**

A definitional grasp of "knowledge" is in order. Kant was a fierce thinker, so we shall rely upon him to illuminate the constitution of knowledge. Before presenting Kant's view of knowledge, it is important to understand the following terms: "subjective" and "objective." Subjectivity is a reference to one's experience excluding how others experience the same phenomenon. Objectivity occurs when there are parallel perceptions of similar experiences among people. Subjectivity applies to personal evaluation of personal experience. Objectivity applies when others draw the same conclusion in an identical context without personal bias.

> Opinion is a consciously insufficient judgment, subjectively as well as objectively. Belief is subjectively sufficient, but is recognized as being objectively insufficient. Knowledge is both subjectively and objectively sufficient.   **KANT 8**

When opinion is more popular than fact, the tendency to ascribe events and circumstances to chance, increases. When "happening" deviates from our opinions, we shrug our shoulders and resign the incident to accident. Chance is the catch-all reservoir for prolonged uncertainty and an unreasoning life.

> The only thing that can become fate for a man is belief in fate...   **MARTIN BUBER 9**

Does this imply that we never ascribe situations to chance? During our developmental years we require recourse to vent our frustrations by accepting the idea of accident. As adults, to accept chance as a cause of our choices and their outcome invites superstition, myths and plain foolishness. Frequent recourse to "chance" evidences avoidance of reason or the inability to reason.

> ...ignorance more frequently begets confidence than does knowledge...   **DARWIN 10**

It is all too easy to deny personal responsibility and claim exemption of liability rather than inquire as to the role we play in inducing the outcome. Only tough-minded reasoning and perseverance expose the forerunners to disagreeable events. For example, a male who batters a female betrays an undeveloped or even damaged anima (his feminine principle). A "chances are" perspective seeks justification claiming he was momentarily beside himself (artifice designed to reduce his liability). Physical, emotional and psychological beatings are complex issues. Both sexes are challenged to resolve this low level approach to differences.

> ...it is not of the least service to mankind, nor to either of the two sexes, whether it be that which abuses or that which is abused.   **MONTESQUIEU 11**

Montesquieu's view seems harsh; nonetheless, it is worthy of consideration. Violence is far too popular. No democracy retains noteworthy freedoms without individual liability for acts of cruelty. How substantial can freedom be when psychotic behavior becomes more and more commonplace? As adults, one act of violence against the body of another (murder, rape, beatings and torture), is sufficient indication of the potential for future acts of violence. Mercy, leniency and forgiveness should be extended to the perpetrator only if s/he can prove convincingly and conclusively that s/he will not repeat reprehensible behavior. Until we as a nation become serious in our effort to reduce violence, criminal acts and criminal thinking will accelerate.

> ...in things bereft of reason, there is neither voluntary nor involuntary.   **THOMAS AQUINAS 12**

The development of reason occurs by voluntary, selective choice. Without reason, chance prevails. What kind of life is it when our decisions have no greater basis than the outcome of the toss of a coin?

Without a core of intelligent individuals whose ability to reason is geared to preserve realistic freedom, we will remain subject to the whims and wiles of aberrancy. A lack of reasoning capacity guarantees the failure of society and government to come to grips with newly emerging challenges.

> Either people will remain stultified by a confused range of opinions, or they will accept the opinion of an expert elite   (**RAYMOND B. CATTELL**, *Personal Communication*).

Human beings learn best by example. The goal of an expert elite is to provide an illustration of that which has a proven track record. An expert elite does not coerce individuals to live in a certain manner; they promulgate the best of knowledge. People have the responsibility to make wise choices; unaware of intelligent choices, we suffer the consequences. No one escapes.

1) We respond poorly when others lord it over us.
2) We are not turned on by lording it over others.
3) Do not obstruct or deny us access to the best of knowledge.

The above three comments exemplify the spirit of Cattell's "Personal Communication" regarding the role of "an expert elite."

> Science is the great antidote to the poison of enthusiasm and superstition; and where all the superior ranks of people were secured from it, the inferior ranks could not be much exposed to it.   **ADAM SMITH 13**

Although enthusiasm is a desirable trait, here it refers to excitement which is blind and without foundation. The poison of superstition continues to work magic in spite of modern education. Furthermore, "educated" people today are prone to self-deception and simultaneously, capable of deceiving others. Without standards, years of academic activity tend more toward confused and deceptive thinking rather than reason based on solid attainment.

Until approximately 1960, academia provided an environment which encouraged the development of a few solid and deep thinkers; today we rarely encounter an academician capable of both specific and comprehensive insights.

We tend to reward knowledge in special fields like law,

medicine and football rather than knowledge in general
(**RAYMOND B. CATTELL**, *Personal Communication*).

We must not forget that vast national resources are spent to support academia: grants, salaries, fellowships, buildings, libraries and student loans, to name a few. Academia has made minimal lasting contributions relative to nearly unchecked resources during the past thirty years. Take for example the schools of social work. Since the days of President Lyndon Johnson, the combined efforts of academic social work have failed to effect permanent change in a positive direction for the social ills of America. It is honorable to provide assistance in fulfilling legitimate needs which lead to self-actualization; it is an entirely different matter to encourage people to get what they can simply because it is available. To exploit the attainable because it is legal and available is not always wise. This practice catches up with us; life itself demands a price.

Presently four out of ten Americans regularly receive a government check for some form of support. Is this a reason to be proud as an American? Is this what our forefathers had in mind? A body of professionals with degrees of higher education in social work, pose as experts. These experts and professionals are part of the problem of America's social ills. Their thinking is not very different from those whose efforts to stave off starvation in Africa fail to provide a lasting change which alters the cause of starvation.

The fact is, in a majority of cases, people and their governments cause famines, not nature, not climate
(**JAMES P. GRANT**, *Executive Director of UNICEF*). 14

Efforts in the name of compassion commonly increase suffering and cruelty in the long-term. In many instances, momentary relief leads to an increase in the birthrate of undernourished infants over and above that which occurs without aid. Good intentions and meddling in the affairs of others are unacceptable if we fail to take responsibility for long-term effects. By the same standard, programs which pay child support for an unlimited number of children (simply on the basis of the mother being unmarried), are not compassionate programs. Programs which support immorality and perpetuate delinquency, are not in the national interest. When it comes to tackling complex issues, few people are trained to ask the right questions and provide solid solutions useful for both the present and the future.

> For the human mind is wont to fall into error in two ways here; it either assumes more than is really given in determining the question, or on the other hand, leaves something out. **DESCARTES 15**

Our generation is not between the devil and the deep blue sea due to a lack of knowledge; today's plight of social ills stems directly from the inability to apply knowledge beneficially not only for today, but also, without sowing seeds that increase tomorrow's ills. When knowledge is not applied intelligently, the result leads to destruction. Learning how to obtain welfare aid has the potential of destroying our hope for becoming self-respecting citizens, especially if the check is taken for granted. An attitude of complacency claims handouts as an inherent right.

Certain kinds of ignorance are sometimes useful (ignorance of how to file for welfare aid, for example). We are against welfare when it contributes to ineptitude and lack of ambition (which may apply to a significant number of welfare recipients).

> ...to be helped to help themselves, if they are physically capable of it, is the only charity which proves to be charity in the end. **J.S. MILL 16**

Many welfare recipients deep within their hearts and minds curse having developed dependence on aid. They know far better than those who have never been on welfare what it has <u>not</u> done for them. Their lives provide evidence of its debilitating effect. The tragedy of welfare: once accustomed to its philosophy, it is next to impossible to return to self-reliance.

> If Truth, if knowledge, does not lead to goodness or use of it, which is its genuine partner, for what reason should we seek to study any Truth or knowledge? Knowledge is endless unless it leads to its own goal, which is its goodness. **M. NICOLL 17**

Leaving social work aside let us take a hard look at academic psychology. In the year 2020, retrospectively looking at the years 1960-1989, it is the opinion of this writer that one psychologist, Raymond B. Cattell, will stand alone as having made significant and enduring contributions in the field of clinical psychology. Most other "psychological" contributions will fall by the wayside as fads and titillating notions. How do we explain this? Cattell is keenly aware of history and its relationship to human beings during the past three thousand years. He demands that psychologists rely on measurement in the treatment of their problems as chemistry did when it superseded alchemy. <u>His major concern today is the survival of the human race</u>. Survival does not depend on avoiding nuclear holocaust as much as it depends on maintaining competition within and among groups. Without competition, evolution dies.

Cattell has coined the term "Beyondism," which refers to the need of each group to pioneer and risk its survival by going beyond the present, especially genetically.

> Beyondism says that present mankind is obsolete
> (**RAYMOND B. CATTELL**, *Personal Communication*).

For additional reference of Beyondism, see Cattell's <u>A New Morality From Science</u>: <u>Beyondism</u>. (1972). New York: Pergamon. Also, see: <u>Beyondism</u>: <u>Religion From Science</u>. (1987). New York: Praeger.

Psychology today functions primarily as a babysitter. Little is progressive within academic psychology which we did not already know in 1960. Therapy as a tool has not advanced with the exception of group and family therapy. A slight increase in more highly qualified therapists today than in 1960, is offset by a great increase in less qualified therapists. Psychiatrists, counsellors, psychologists, social workers and clergy fall within the category of "therapist." Therapists resist acknowledging the lack of therapeutic progress for an obvious reason: their livelihood depends upon the continuation of the practice of therapy. One research study found that 60% of patients showed no improvement after a six month follow-up, 20% improved and 20% were worse off after therapy. Quality therapy can contribute to emotional growth and stability; unfortunately, the odds of finding a quality therapist are poor. Besides, therapy as an institution has not advanced to keep pace with the complexities and challenges of modern-day living. For this reason, therapy is reduced to the status of babysitter.

To a certain extent, the lack of progress in standard fare psychology and social work can be attributed to the diminution of the individual. Psychology can never progress beyond the manifestation of the true individual. To an outsider, psychologists and social workers appear as masters of individuality. Many of them have simply adopted the mentality of their respective group and are therapists in spite of arrested development.

> ...for it (Beyondism) recognizes that an important fraction of social progress arises from thought processes which reach their greatest originality in an individual.
>
> **R.B. CATTELL** 18

There is abundant knowledge of psychology, far more than we are presently using effectively. And, there is an increase in social ills, far more than we can afford to live with. Our contention is that ignorance and sentimentality are winning the race against an evolutionary application and integration of knowledge. In area after area we now possess greatly expanded knowledge. Lamentably, the abundance of knowledge is not producing minds capable of leading us into the twenty-first century. Most important, we are not progressing in human relationships—husband and wife, parent and child, employer and employee.

REFERENCES

1. Bergler, E. (1961). *Counter-feit sex: homosexuality, impotence, frigidity.* New York: Grove Press. Page ix.

2. Kant. Volume 42. Page 175.

3. Hume. Volume 35. Page 488.

4. Cattell, R.B. (1972). *A new morality from science: Beyondism.* New

York: Pergamon. Page 110.

5. Plotinus. Volume 17. Page 350.

6. Kant. Volume 42. Page 230.

7. Machiavelli. Volume 23. Page 78.

8. Kant. Volume 42. Page 241.

9. Buber, M. (1958). *I and thou.* New York: Charles Scribner's Sons. Page 57.

10. Darwin. Volume 49. Page 253.

11. Montesquieu. Volume 38. Page 117.

12. Aquinas, T. Volume 19. Page 650.

13. Smith, Adam. Volume 39. Page 347.

14. "Nature not worst culprit of famine." San Diego Union 23 February 1988. Page 1.

15. Descartes. Volume 31. Page 26.

16. Mill, J.S. (1970). *The subjection of women.* Cambridge and London: The M.I.T. Press. Page 88.

17. Nicoll, M. (1950). *The new man.* London: Vincent Stuart. Page 49.

18. Cattell, R.B. (1987). *Beyondism: religion from science.* New York: Praeger. Page 278.

CHAPTER FIVE

TRUTH vs. FALSEHOOD

I f falsehood had, like <u>truth</u>, but one face only, we should be upon better terms; for we should then take for certain the contrary to what the liar says: but the reverse of <u>truth</u> has a hundred thousand forms, and a field indefinite, without bound or limit.   **MONTAIGNE 1**

Pilate asked Jesus, "What is truth?" and Jesus replied, "You shall know the truth and the truth shall make you free." From the response we can conclude: 1) truth is knowable, and 2) truth promotes freedom. Something within "truth" makes us free. Whatever does not lead to or result in freedom is false. Falsehood results in slavery (of another) or enslavement (of myself). The expression "you shall know the truth" indicates a process which requires time. Each life experience can be put to a test: does it move in the direction of freedom or away from freedom?

Many spend a lifetime seeking truth. They look everywhere for truth: toward the planets, inside churches, in the nucleus of cells, in foreign countries; everywhere, except deep within themselves. The <u>cult</u> of truth-seeking dodges a sincere relationship with that which is true. What is "that which is true?" One example is the fact that any life history is unalterable at the moment of entering our grave. We could have said death; rather we say grave because the image of grave entails a covering-up (burial) of life on this earth. Each "life" includes all thoughts, feelings, and actions, and equally significant—all thoughts, feelings, and actions never experienced. The meaning of death is fulfilled with the burial of a specific life history. This is undeniably true; the content of a life history at the time of death is irrevocable. This brings to mind the definition of philosophy found in the works of Plato: meditation upon death.

Truth can be heady and high-minded; let us begin with basics—ourselves. The medium for understanding the bare essentials regarding truth is our mind. A major function of our mind is reasoning. Proper reasoning seeks out principles. The merit of principle lies in its elimination of exceptions to the rule. Rules simplify the recognition of contradiction.

The first principle of proper reasoning calls for clear and specific meaning accorded to words (symbols of language).

> ...when words are used without a meaning, you may put them together as you please without danger of running into a contradiction.   **BERKELEY**

Without meaning there is no truth; meaning provides context, whereby truth is known.

A carpenter cuts a piece of lumber for a specific opening. When the wood fits snugly, it can be described as having a good fit. All other lengths of wood (longer and shorter) possess no specific meaning for the opening. Truth is like the snug fit of wood insofar as it requires a specific application in a particular context. It need not be perfect (a slightly shorter piece of lumber works), but it must be at least adequate. Picture one hundred pieces of wood of varied lengths. For a specific opening, only three out of one hundred pieces fit adequately. One is slightly loose, another fits snugly and the third must be hammered into place.

Earlier it was stated that truth need not be perfect. This statement arouses great anxiety and suspicion among spiritual babes whose sense of security depends on the categories of black and white. Where there are human beings there are imperfections. A great distance lies between striving toward perfection and demanding unattainable perfection. Only vain and unseasoned individuals demand perfection. It is one thing to strive and improve, and quite another matter to demand perfection of others.

Truth qualifies as truth provided it is comprehensively adequate even though it is not perfect. Proof for this is the fact that truth derives its meaning through the channel of the human mind (in spite of our imperfect human minds).

An assumption, "what is true for me may not be true for the next individual" is oft repeated. This sounds intelligent and has great appeal, as it comes disguised as an argument full of generosity and liberalism. Underlying the aforementioned assumption is a refusal to come to grips with truth for myself. As long as we can hide by insisting upon diversity between our truth and our neighbor's truth, we are not compelled to identify truth as it relates to ourselves. This smacks of cowardice. "No two people think alike" does not contradict mutual understanding of principle. What the first statement of this paragraph really says is: my unprincipled mind can never accord with your unprincipled mind. Jesus said we shall know the truth. Imagine Jesus saying: "what is true for me may not be true for my neighbor." Is truth suddenly evident? No. At the same time, we must rid ourselves of an attitude which makes the apprehension of truth impossible.

Montaigne said that truth has but one face only. Differences in understanding what is true originate with inadequacies of our minds. Our differences are not the result of fluctuating truth.

> As to past Experience, it can be allowed to give direct and certain information of those precise objects only, and that precise period of time, which fell under its cognizance... **DAVID HUME** 3

Truth does not fluctuate (that which fluctuates is true to its fluctuation), for truth is apprehension of a specific at a set point in time. Our thinking vacillates when we maintain contradictory viewpoints.

Erroneous notions resist the identification and comprehension of truth. This resistance consolidates an attitude whereby our culture backslides in distancing itself from the effort of specifying and understanding truth. The result: we are but a step away from losing altogether the art of distinguishing between something true and something false. A change in attitude is necessary from "what is true for me may not be true for the next individual," to: 1) we are unable to agree upon the meaning of an event, or, 2) our ability to communicate is inadequate for mutual comprehension.

> ...Truth cannot apply to something conflicting with itself; what it affirms it must also be. **PLOTINUS** 4

One of the surest ways for so-called truth to conflict with itself is through the presentation of uncertain language. Should we desire to speak truthfully, it is necessary that our speech be unambiguous and comprehensible.

A true fit of wood calls for a minimum of slack. Some may respond, "if truth is tolerant of adjustment, then nobody speaks the truth." "Adjustment" must fit within the limitation of adequate. Assumptions and confusion would be greatly reduced if we acknowledged our ignorance. Often we hide in the gray area of pretending to know, claiming to speak truth, when we ought to speak the truth of our uncertainty.

> Which insufficiency of language, though I cannot note it
> for false philosophy, yet it hath a quality, not only to hide
> the truth, but also to make men think they have it, and
> desist from further search.   **THOMAS HOBBES 5**

Self-deception is the easiest thing in the world. The other extreme occurs when we know the truth and willfully conceal it.

Thus far we observe that truth . . .
1) makes us free.
2) has no meaning when disconnected from our mind.
3) is comprehensively adequate.
4) is not self-conflicting.
5) lends itself to clear communication.

A chapter on truth would be incomplete without addressing truth and religion.

> The notion that it is one man's duty that another should
> be religious, was the foundation of all the religious
> persecutions ever perpetrated.   **J.S. MILL 6**

Three individuals worship God by different methods. Each person is uncomfortable with the methodology for worship of the other two. Insecurity and paranoia demand that others believe as we do and worship in the manner we worship.

> ...the chief stronghold of our hypocrisy [is] to be ever
> judging one another.   **JOHN MILTON 7**

Ideal worship is imaginary. It is impossible for any human being to worship God perfectly; the difference between man and God is incomprehensibly great.

It is the customary fate of new truths to begin as
heresies.   **THOMAS HUXLEY 8**

Truth by revelation is not a number of verses which we cut
out of the Bible and paste on our brain. Revealed truth is of divine
origin. It is recorded so that we may derive meaning and
surrender to spiritual experience.

> Revealed truth may occasionally by luck coincide with
> real truth. For example, most savages forbid incest as a
> revealed truth, but later biology proved it to be correct
> (**RAYMOND B. CATTELL**, *Personal Communication*).

The meaning of truth is not easily perceived, especially
when our culture prefers to dispense with certain qualities, e.g.,
truth, character, dignity, honesty and temperance. If we dis-
agree, when was the last time we heard a serious and enlighten-
ing discussion of these topics on television? Even though certain
notions, e.g., truth, are culturally unpopular and undiscussed,
this ought not bar us from an indepth investigation of the nature
of truth. A readiness to acknowledge a backward slide (regression) is necessary before it is possible to go forward. We are
reminded of a verse in Goethe's "Faust":

> Woe! Woe!
> Thou hast destroyed
> The beautiful world,
> With powerful fist;
> 'Tis smashed, downward hurled!
> A demigod dashed it to bits!
> We're trailing
> The ruins on to the Void,
> And wailing
> Over the beauty lost and gone!
> Mighty one
> Midst the sons of earth,
> Splendider
> Build it again,
> Build it aloft in thy breast!
> And life's new quest
> Commence
> With clearer sense,
> And songs of cheer
> Anew shalt hear!   **9**

Many innocent individuals are turned off by the idea of truth; in the name of "truth" we have been deceived and taken advantage of all too frequently. Meaningless language (gibberish) is disguised as truth.

A strong identification with the personality of another individual results in many believing unquestioningly what they are told. Unaware of pitfalls, we become ensnared by the charisma of a personality rather than observe the absence of substance. A personality is substituted for "truth" when we believe a speaker who claims possession of truth: "I have the truth; whoever and whatever disagrees with my truth is false." Some preachers go further and claim that disagreement comes from the devil. Religious experience is often no more than the worship of a personality—personality being that of the speaker.

Serious inquiry is laborious. Persistent inquiry (particularly in matters of religion and science), is indispensable for today's complex world.

> There are in the human mind two very distinct forces, one inspiring the need to believe, the other the need to inquire. Neither of these faculties should be favored at the expense of the other. **MADAME DE STAEL 10**

There are no limits to the steps people take in order to avoid the labor of serious thinking. The habit of a penetrating mind is created through uncertainty, error and perseverance. No one is born a profound thinker. A self-motivated child (through exercise of his/her mind) potentially develops strong mental faculties as an adult. Belief without inquiry supports the increase of myths, superstitions, illusions and falsehood.

The experience of truth varies with each generation's demand for truth. By accepting falsehood, we "successfully" avoid the pain of deep thinking. Avoidance of serious thinking equates with illusion-embrace.

> It is a truism to say that we always pay painfully in the end for the falsity of our comforting illusions, but it is also a psychological truism that humans prefer the nearer satisfactions of a myth to the remoter goals of truth. **R.B. CATTELL 11**

> Truth, such as is necessary to the regulation of life, is always found where it is honestly sought. **S. JOHNSON 12**

Momentarily consider an alternative: Truth, such as is necessary to the regulation of life, is rarely found where it is honestly sought. We may be offended because "always" is replaced with "rarely" and we insist upon a middle road: "sometimes found" and "sometimes not found." This position reveals resistance to truth. "Sometimes yes" and sometimes no" is fifty percent of the time and once again we have regressed to the toss of a coin. It is written in the beginning of this chapter "truth need not be perfect." Only three pieces of wood (out of one hundred) adequately fit the opening; the other ninety-seven do not fit. There is a great difference between the randomness of 50% and the elimination of 97 pieces of wood which do not fit the opening. We practice a random approach to life , particularly in deciding which ideas to believe. For example, commonly we hear, "if it feels good, do it." This limited approach does not take into consideration that what feels good today may result in a cessation of feeling and an increase of frustration, tomorrow. "I'll try anything once" is another random approach. A random selection rarely results in a true fit.

A navigator follows a series of principles in order to come to port. Not only does he seek to arrive at a specific port, he also aims to arrive by a set time. Random navigation does not aim at a particular port; neither is there an intended time of arrival (assuming that we arrive at all).

Uncertainty precedes principle. Patience is a prerequisite for identifying principles. The purpose of uncertainty is not to promote randomness; the goal is to move in the direction of recognizing principles.

> Uncertainty is admittedly widespread, but the sincerity of a truth-seeker is judged by the efforts he makes to reduce it. One may suspect other motives than truth-seeking in those who worship, prolong and perpetuate uncertainty. **R.B. CATTELL 13**

Uncertainty is an admission of ignorance, not a license to wander aimlessly. The goal of trial by error is to attain certainty. Error is an essential fact of life, without which we do not live. Unchecked error engenders traumatic living. By reducing error we begin to establish principles. Uncertainty is not to be denigrated when it leads to principle. The value of principle lies in its contribution to stability.

> Experience shows that some understand more deeply
> than do others, as one who carries a conclusion to its first
> principles and ultimate causes understands it more
> deeply than the one who reduces it only to its proximate
> causes.   **THOMAS AQUINAS 14**

This finding elucidates misunderstandings between individuals. To begin with, each party to a greater or lesser extent is aware of the total picture. Also, the personal agenda factor prevents us from viewing other perspectives.

The beauty of initial uncertainty is to guard against the pretense of claiming to know all there is to know. This applies to both religion and science.

Initial uncertainty can lead to scientific understanding. Likewise, uncertainty in religious matters keeps us from murdering our neighbor (in thought) and allows us to accept devotion to God as a personal experience without violating our neighbor's experience of devotion or lack thereof. Only a tested zealot of character can withstand the temptation to make demands of others in religious matters. I have experienced the burning urge to spread everywhere the fervor of my religious conviction. In retrospect, I acknowledge my fervor to have been a fever of personal insecurity, uncertainty, and inadequacy.

Every day the battleline is drawn between the true and the false. How do we distinguish between appearance and substance? There must be a developmental skill which leads to principle. Plato believed the art of measurement cuts through the facade of appearance. In the world of science, there are instruments which measure with microscopic accuracy. Measurement is to science what judgment is to human beings. Remove measurement and there is no science; remove judgment and we eliminate human beings. Scientific measurement requires clear and level-headed thinking which insists upon precision. Judgment (conclusion based upon observation and experience), falls into two categories: correct or faulty. There is no incorrect scientific measurement. Plato recognized the challenge of accurate measurement, hence he specified "the art of measurement." Accurate measurement requires time and has the potential of becoming scientific. Good judgment is formed by trial and error (which takes time and requires wisdom). Initial uncertainty prevents premature and inaccurate conclusions (poor judgment); prolonged uncertainty reveals a lack of interest in coming to grips with guidelines.

Nietzsche devoted his lifetime distinguishing between truth and falsehood. He upset the status quo and became the enemy of many during the second half of the nineteenth century. Jesus also became the enemy of many, but on a grander scale. Our aim is not to compare Nietzsche and Jesus; it is to expose great resistance to truth in all ages.

> In theory it is easy to convince an ignorant person; but in the affairs of real life no one offers himself to be convinced, and we hate the man who has convinced us.
> **EPICTETUS 15**

By resisting opportunities to learn from others, it is next to impossible to develop the ability to distinguish truth from falsehood. Is it not true that a learned individual acquires insights, knowledge and truisms from others? We not only must acquire, but more importantly, integrate acquisitions. It is the ability to integrate which provides the cutting edge for creating awareness of truth.

> 'Truth' is therefore not something there, that might be found or discovered—but something that must be created...
> **NIETZSCHE 16**

'Truth' which we fail to acknowledge does not exist. It is one accomplishment to identify truth, it is wholly a different matter to know how to put the knowledge of truth into operation (truth in creation). Awareness of truth has negative value until it is put to use. For example, an individual with a high IQ has a great capacity for making contributions to the present and future generations. Of what value is the high IQ "truth" when it is narrowly employed, destructively employed (to self and others) or never activated?

Possession of sufficient money for the essentials in life combined with high standards of thinking, far surpass a mad push for unlimited wealth with zero focus on the spiritual quality of our life. Better yet would be an abundance of wealth linked to the commitment to add quality to everyone's life. Regrettably, rarely does anybody possess sufficient character to withstand foolish spending and misguided efforts, when money is not an object. Am I suggesting that poverty be made a virtue? The doom of poverty is as lacking in virtue as a wealthy individual who lacks strength of character. Both conditions are impoverished.

Vacations are necessary, but who would boast of a vacation which contributes to mental deterioration? It is one thing to vacate our minds—free ourselves from the daily rat race—it is quite another to reinforce bad habits which in the end evince dull and wayward minds.

> The charm of leisure must not be indolent vacancy of mind, but the investigation or discovery of truth, that thus every man may make solid attainments without grudging that others do the same. **AUGUSTINE 17**

If the preceding comment turns us off, then we possess indolent minds. St. Augustine's expression "solid attainments" parallels Nietzsche's "creation of truth."

Ethical standards unite the spirit of the law and the letter of the law. Strict adherence to the letter of the law results in an unthinking approach, for example, obedience for the sake of obeying. Personal responsibility is strengthened by awareness of the letter and the spirit of the law. Rigorous obedience to the letter of the law does not absolve us of further liability. To take the view that you will obey the law and that others must be responsible for the outcome, portrays a closed or feeble mind.

Knowing how to distinguish between the letter and the spirit of the law adds meaning to religious belief. The letter of the law insists upon the recognition of a higher power. The spirit of the law in religious matters requires personal responsibility in implementing devotion. Of course there are agnostic objections. An agnostic (one who claims it is impossible to know how to be responsible in matters of devotion), is analogous to a man who dates fifty women and fails to choose one woman with whom to share life. He convinces himself that it is impossible to know which woman is best for him and for whom he would be best. The reverse of this is equally true: the failure of a woman to choose one man to share her life.

What tool do we have to aid our judgment in human relationships? We have intuition, a radar with unlimited possibilities when combined with body language, speech and eye movement. Our eyes and body reveal the continuity or discontinuity of our thoughts. Inconsistencies of speech and eye movement expose lies or reveal contradictions. Intuitive radar is of great value in detecting another's attempt to lie, misrepresent, or plan evil. Freud developed high-powered radar enabling him to draw deductions on human behavior. His conclusions disturbed the general population (primarily in the western world), for about a century.

In human interaction, human radar is the most valuable tool in pointing up falsehood and deception. Human radar pinpoints the intersection of contradiction. Jesus taught:

> The light of the body is the eye: if therefore thine eye be single, thy whole body shall be full of light.
>
> **(Matthew 6:22)** 18

A single eye is capable of sharp focus in a single direction. Undivided attention is a consistent eye, one which does not misrepresent, nor is it torn between two or more possibilities. This is what the psychologist calls validity and reliability of a test.

Matthew 6:22, when applied to romance leads to the following recognition: mutually cherished romance embodies undivided participation of both parties, who understand that all romance external to their situation can not subtract from the beauty of their experience.

A blinding limitation of our human radar is the inability to detect lies (untruths) in others which we have come to accept as "truths" for ourselves.

As children we are trained to approach truth as a black and white issue. Either we took the candy or we did not take the candy. Either we told the truth or we did not tell the truth. As adults, we become aware at some point that truth and falsehood are not so easily distinguished. Aristotle taught that what is true or false involves a synthesis of concepts. Aristotle's viewpoint does not contradict black and white simplicity. Aristotle presumes that we advance from our childhood level of understanding. In leaving our childhood, the abandonment of innocence and simplicity is ill-advised. Aristotle's "synthesis of concepts" in ascertaining truth or falsehood is not an invitation to incorporate subterfuge, deceit and misrepresentation. Honesty is always essential in determining what is true or false.

The habit of speaking the truth and honest thinking contribute to the quality of our lives. We are attracted to one another to a great extent on the basis of similarities, particularly along lines of integrity. The habit of lying to ourselves and others, deceiving ourselves and others, attracts "friends" who are also accustomed to dishonesty. In the long run, those who are familiar with honest thinking and sincere speaking, experience less psychological trauma (in spite of retaining higher levels of innocence, which translate into greater susceptibility to being duped), than those accustomed to fraud and chicanery. Jesus said truth shall be known.

TRUTH:
1) promotes freedom.
2) has no meaning when disconnected from the human mind.
3) is comprehensively adequate.
4) is not self-conflicting.
5) lends itself to clear communication.
6) is not a personality.
7) is consistent with principle.
8) does not yield to a random approach.
9) shows itself best through careful measurement.
10) is created with the aid of serious inquiry.

REFERENCES

1. Montaigne. Volume 25. Page 16.

2. Berkeley. Volume 35. Page 428.

3. Hume. Volume 35. Page 461.

4. Plotinus. Volume 17. Page 218.

5. Machiavelli. Volume 23. Page 274.

6. Mill, J.S. Volume 43. Page 311.

7. Milton. Volume 32. Pages 409-410.

8. *The World Book Dictionary* (1972). Spoken by Thomas Huxley. Found under "heresy." Chicago: Doubleday.

9. Goethe. Volume 47. Page 39.

10. de Stael, Madame (1964). *On politics, literature and national character.* Garden City, New York: Doubleday. Page 335.

11. Cattell, R.B. (1987). *Beyondism: religion from science.* New York: Praeger. Page 78.

12. Johnson, S. (1759, 1976). *The history of Rasselas, prince of abissinia.* New York: Penguin Books. Page 58.

13. Cattell, R.B. (1972). *A new morality from science: Beyondism.* New York: Pergamon. Page 317.

14. Aquinas, T. Volume 19. pp. 459-460.

15. Epictetus. Volume 12. Page 132.

16. Schacht, R. (1983). *Nietzsche.* London: Routledge & Kegan Paul. Page 109.

17. Augustine. Volume 18. Page 523.

18. The Holy Bible. London: Oxford University Press.

19. Montesquieu. Volume 38. Page 14.

CHAPTER SIX

LEADERSHIP vs. ANARCHY

The Greek root for anarchy means leaderless. When we hear the term "leader," what thoughts come to mind? A great person of the past, dictator, someone who inspires, dispenser of orders, somebody who refuses to understand mercy, or an individual who is compassionate? Leaders have been portrayed in many forms and disguises throughout history. Different eras require and foster varied types of leaders.

The twentieth century is drawing to a close. What kind of leader does today's global world require?

Leadership is built upon the strength within an individual, not upon the weak-mindedness of groups. A case in point is King Victor Manuel of Italy during the nineteenth century. The people demanded King Victor Manuel as their leader against the Austrians praising him as saviour. Later, they (including Elizabeth Barret Browning), were very angry because he didn't do anything.

"Strength" in leadership can be resolved by high A, F, and G (A—outgoing, F—happy-go-lucky and G—conscientious) on the 16pf (a personality test of 16 factors developed by Raymond B. Cattell). The best leader is not proud of leading followers but strives to develop leadership qualities in followers.

"Leadership" in America must reconsider interpretations of democracy which advocate rights and freedoms without responsibility. Democratic notions which end in anarchy begin by eliminating standards. For early Americans, aristocracy was an extreme form of government with too many restrictions and limitations for the people. Conversely, present American democracy is an extreme form of government engaged in removing standards. Indulgent leadership is what most liberals want. Leadership whose object is the preservation of democracy must find a way to restore standards and greatness in America. Present democratic ideals work against progress.

> Do not great crimes and the spirit of pure evil spring out of a fulness of nature ruined by education rather than from any inferiority, whereas weak natures are scarcely capable of any very great good or very great evil?
>
> SOCRATES 1

Our present system of education fails to create strong character in students. Leadership recognizes that it is futile at present to expect either religion or the home to provide strong character development in the citizens of America. Both have failed and neither will fulfill in the near future what has been their historical role. The permanent abandonment of church and home as places of character development is not recommended. However, our nation has fallen so far behind in character development that the media and schools must take responsibility for reintroducing and reinforcing character development.

The Emotional-Cognitive Law states that thinking ability is only as good as emotional stability. Emotionally unstable pupils disrupt the learning process of a group. Cognitive emphasis is a waste of time until minimal emotional stability is acquired. Children lacking in self-restraint (beginning in kindergarten) should spend an entire year focusing on emotional development. This is not a democratic idea, but it has the potential of altering self-defeating habits of pupils and cutting in half the future number of criminals. Here is an instance when democratic ideals should be sacrificed in the interest of safeguarding our future.

Democracy is concerned with giving everybody an education; a progressive nation is compelled to know what kind of education citizens are receiving and insists upon quality education.

We are living in a world of unmitigating fluctuation. For the first time in the history of human beings, transitions in thought, technology, lifestyles, transportation and communication are so rapid that only gifted minds comprehend the shifting. These unprecedented phenomena require the utmost in foresight for our present leaders.

> We must recall, in support, that mankind would never get anywhere with leaders who love it as it is, but only those who are benevolent to the coming man.
>
> R.B. CATTELL 2

When situations change without advance notice, looking into the future is as important as immediate problem solving. Solving today's problems while simultaneously anticipating tomorrow's difficulties is necessary in a world which resists stabilization. The present lack of leadership is evident in the effort to solve endless problems with only temporary solutions. Leaders can not afford to be short-sighted like the contented surfer whose vision of a forthcoming tsunami is obstructed by a series of small waves.

> ...a permissive society prefers to avoid immediate difficulties at the cost of graver ones ahead.
>
> R.B. CATTELL 3

Significant proof that America is burdened with a permissive society is evident in the gutless debates of our Congress which resists budget cutting notwithstanding our crippling deficit.

David Stockman was the Budget Director for the Office of Management and Budget from January, 1980 to August, 1985. Stockman foresaw the unprecedented escalation of the deficit, due to the administration's irresponsible economic rationalizations. Like any responsible prophet, he blew the whistle time and time again warning of impending disaster. In the darkness of night, Stockman was a lighthouse beaming warnings to our economic Ship of State. He refused to join the rank and file whose daily efforts could be summed up as "figures lie and liars figure." The October, 1987 stock market crash momentarily exposed the precarious nature of statistical manipulation and economic indicators.

Almost two centuries ago, Madame de Stael denounced Napoleon's unending military conquests. Napoleon exiled her more than once. Stockman could easily join Madame de Stael in her comment:

> Throughout my life the errors I have made in politics

have stemmed from the idea that men could always be moved by the truth if it was presented to them vigorously.   **MADAME DE STAEL 4**

See Stockman's <u>Triumph of Politics</u>, (1986) Harper & Row: New York, for an intriguing account of budget activities from January, 1980 to August, 1985. Stockman's knowledge of economics led to the understanding that there are limits to subtle economic reasoning designed to deceive.

Today's leaders must possess great courage and be able to withstand the pressure of special interest groups and mass-mind persuasion. Groups are often quite successful in obtaining their objectives simply because of their numbers and their capacity to make noise.

For the most part our leaders are merely following out in front; they do but marshal us the way we are going.
                                    BERGEN EVANS 5

Artifice and charisma are often misconstrued as evidence of leadership. The need to rely upon deception and camouflage reveals a lack of sincerity. Genuine leadership is noted by its authenticity and guidance.

If, without reflection, we can be led into a given situation, what prevents others from taking us another direction? True leadership results in followers internalizing motives and values of a particular cause and direction.

LEADERSHIP . . .
1) recognizes that today's rate of change is unprecedented.
2) plugs the dike today while reducing recurring leaks tomorrow.
3) avoids future disaster by adopting austere measures whenever necessary.
4) requires self-control.

He who has never learned to obey cannot be a good commander.   **ARISTOTLE 6**

Strength of character is inseparable from self-mastery. Disciplined thought and reliable behavior combine to form character. Without the guiding strength of principle and character, it is difficult to define trustworthy leadership.

> Of all the difficulties which impede the progress of
> thought, and the formation of well-grounded opinions of
> life and social arrangements, the greatest is now the
> unspeakable ignorance and inattention of mankind in
> respect to the influences which form human character.
>
> **J.S. MILL** 7

Strength of leadership does not begin with a crisis; a crisis requires individuals who already possess the qualities of leadership. Individuals who demonstrate leadership in time of crisis possess a background in strength of character. Take the example of Abraham Lincoln who led our country through its worst crisis. Lincoln's success can, to a great extent, be attributed to his powerful strength of character, dating back to his childhood days, which provided the backbone for his relentless conviction of "save the Union whatever the cost."

The distinguished social scientist, Dr. Raymond B. Cattell, informs us:

> ...education of the emotions and the building of charac-
> ter are probably the more important half of education.
>
> 8

True leaders can identify weak character and the lack of discerning intelligence. Our first priority in returning to the status of a first-rate and internally powerful nation requires strong national character. This requires the development of sturdy individual character.

What hinders the development of character? To begin with, permissive parents fail to set standards for emotional maturity. By contrast, the British public schools put character development ahead of academic learning. Trustworthy character requires emotional maturity.

In the past, the "do your own thing" philosophy frequently resulted in positive results. Today, "do your own thing" often translates into an increase in individuals who are idiosyncratic and without character. "Do my own thing" is now as unproductive for leadership development as is the passive decision to do nothing—let others lead. Both approaches seek to eliminate personal responsibility. By letting others lead, we invite dupes (followers) to be led by dupes ("leaders") when neither has a clue as to their destination. Small wonder today's younger generation is insecure and confused.

> It is not the young people that degenerate; they are not
> spoiled till those of maturer age are already sunk into
> corruption.   **MONTESQUIEU 9**

A barrage of arguments seek to counter Montesquieu's view.
A likely argument runs: "through peer pressure, young people
acquire their trashy habits and ideas." Do children create
television programming? Do children establish school curriculum? Do children set the standards and establish cultural
direction? Children inherit television programming, school cur-
riculums and cultural trends from present and past generations.
The slack hand of permissive parents encourages children to self-
indulge.

The failure to set standards leads to no standards. Leadership is based upon principles, not whim. The habit of passivity is
at the mercy of whichever direction the wind blows.

> Yet the habit of passive acceptance is a disastrous one in
> later life. It causes men to seek a leader, and to accept
> as a leader whoever is established in that position.
>   **B. RUSSELL 10**

The word "obey" has its roots in a Latin term meaning "to
hear." Noses turn up at the word obedience (presently a word of
uncertain reputation). This is due in great part to the abuse
obedient individuals have suffered. Far too often we obeyed those
who lorded it over us while they took advantage of our ignorance.
Adding insult to injury, we were called wimps. It is important
that we discern when to listen and obey, and when to disregard.
Blind obedience in today's fast and changing world carries treach-
erous consequences. Recall the Jim Jones incident in Guyana.
Certainly this is an extreme example, but it does make a point.
Personal leadership is requisite for a life worth living.

> And we ought in time of peace from youth upwards to
> practise this habit of commanding others, and of being
> commanded by others; anarchy should have no place in
> the life of man or of the beasts who are subject to man.
>   **PLATO 11**

Obedience is passive whereas commanding is active. Both
are essential within the same individual. A leader who commands but can not obey, tyrannizes. Tyrants instill fear and
demand obedient followers. Tyranny ought not be confused with

leadership simply because many "leaders"—individuals in positions of power—have been tyrants.

> Empirical studies in leaders in practical situations show they are exceptionally high in A—outgoing, F—happy-go-lucky and G—conscientious, but not so much in E (dominance as people suppose).
> (**RAYMOND B. CATTELL**, *Personal Communication.*)

The greatest leaders of all times have led by example; their example of leadership has value for all ages. Lao-Tse (c. 565 B.C.) provides an illustration:

> A leader is best
> When people barely know he exists.
> Not so good when people obey and acclaim him,
> Worse when they despise him.
> "Fail to honor people,
> They fail to honor you;"
> But of a good leader, who talks little,
> When his work is done, his aim fulfilled,
> They will say, "We did this ourselves." 12

Even though individuals in position of authority have many opportunities to provide examples of leadership, authority does not create leaders. An effective leader identifies issues requiring immediate attention, exhibits personal mastery relevant to the issues and points the way for others to acquire mastery. For example, leaders in education find it necessary to educate themselves beyond the neglect of formalized schooling (bachelor, master and doctoral levels), and acquire the ability to think comprehensively and relevantly. Only then do teachers and professors contribute to the development of creative thinking in their students.

> The reading of great books and the time normally available in other generations for individual thought, reflection, and the formation of independent opinion have inevitably suffered grievously with the crescendo of activity in the mass media. **R. B. CATTELL 13**

The art of true leadership requires a foundation which can stand <u>independent</u> of authority, money, fame and coercion.

We add to our list of leadership qualities:

LEADERSHIP . . .
5) manifests itself through human character.
6) is built upon principle, not whim.
7) obeys and commands.
8) first exercises self-mastery and secondly—points the way.

"Do your own thing" is not government of the people, by the people, and for the people. Endless demands for freedom are of little value when they lead to weakness and destruction. America guarantees personal freedoms, freedoms which are worthless if we fail to maintain standards in line with other leading countries. In a state of war, democratic beliefs are sacrificed one after another.

> The altruism and self-sacrifice which strengthen the group immediately, may weaken it in the long run, if they aid the survival of the weak at the expense of the strong. **R.B. CATTELL 14**

The above quote requires a most careful reading in order to avoid misinterpretation. Does it suggest a discontinuation of altruism and self-sacrifice? Is there a hint to stop giving aid to the weak and poor? Should only the strong be supported? A resounding "NO!" to all of the above. The goal is to reduce the present escalation of suffering. Of what value is it to assist the weak in remaining weak? Welfare and aid must be designed to make the poor less poor, the weak less weak. Most of the poor will never be rich and many of the weak will remain weak; but, as a group the poor and weak do not have to remain hopelessly and unchangeably poor and weak. The economist Ricardo introduced the term "redundant population." Nothing improves from one generation to the next for a redundant population. The present structure of welfare (since 1965) is creating an expanding redundant population. Are we against welfare? Not at all; we are against unprincipled and misdirected welfare aid—welfare aid without a destiny.

> The important question of how poverty is to be abolished is one of the most disturbing problems which agitate modern society. **HEGEL 15**

> The answer to welfare is welfare combined with genetic control
> **(RAYMOND B. CATTELL, Personal Communication).**

We need to take a serious look at the number of children a parent may have when s/he prove to be unfit (by virtue of financial or emotional instability) to provide a minimal suitable home environment. When an inadequate parent continues to reproduce, government might intervene by offering medical procedures that would limit family size. In today's world, a family of two or three is large even for financially, emotionally and mentally stable parents. The above view evokes strong opposition (invasion of rights of privacy, restriction of personal liberties, etc., etc., etc.); nonetheless, we must seriously examine what is presently happening. Government support for two children versus eight to twelve children is a considerable improvement in situations which are inhumane to the children. Tolerating distinctly unqualified parents to have two children, could be viewed as a liberal position.

It is only a matter of time before we acknowledge that a certain portion of state welfare becomes our worst enemy by <u>increasing</u> trauma and poverty and thereby preventing individuals born in this kind of environment from having an opportunity for dignity. Billions upon billions of dollars in the form of aid do not create dignity; high cultural standards lead to dignity. What is the value of life if it can not be cherished? There is joy in all struggles, but to begin life with incredible odds against one is an act of cruelty and should never be supported on a large scale. Continuing to pump dollars into unfortunate, self-perpetuating and degenerating situations is not a viable solution. Foresight is clearly indicated. We have a serious and not easily resolved dilemma on our hands. Ideally, people would self-impose standards. Life is less than ideal.

Government intervention which perpetuates poverty is untenable. Moral responsibility is absent in this arrangement, whether on behalf of government support or on behalf of all human beings who procreate victims.

> The civil libertarian movement needs examination in its notion of privilege without responsibility. The movement says the state shouldn't interfere with privacy; society constantly interferes with crime
> **(RAYMOND B. CATTELL**, *Personal Communication).*

Rights and freedoms made America a powerful nation; they also have the potential to destroy America. With special interest groups, constitutional "rights" screamers (often, nothing more

than the demand for the choice of our indulgence), and confused
thinking extant today; our legislation, administration and juris-
diction of democracy stand in dire need of leadership. Our
thinking is muddled and contradictory in regard to a practical
understanding of privacy, rights, responsibility and freedom.
This ideological confusion receives major support from the vacil-
lating lawyer politician.

> For whereas the lawyer politician hedges every recorded
> statement, to tie him down as little as possible, and often
> to convey promises he has no hope of fulfilling, the aim
> of the scientist is to use language and figures to say as
> pointedly and exactly as possible what he believes the
> truth to be.   **R.B. CATTELL 16**

A leader does not hem and haw. Today's lawyer politician
expends great energy on obtaining votes rather than focusing on
urgent issues and taking an independent stand (which comes
from both his head and heart), regarding those issues. Our
generation of politicians rarely produces a leader.

> ...every one waiting for some bold demonstration from
> his neighbor, in obedience to that innate tendency of
> men, which makes them quick to follow where they are
> slow to lead.   **TACITUS 17**

A strange phenomenon has emerged in American political
leadership. Today's presidential candidate first and foremost
attempts to discover what the people want. Potential "leaders"
mirror the wants and desires of the voters.

> In short, the whole art of those great politicians lies in so
> mesmerising those they stand in need of, they each may
> think he is laboring for his own interest in working for
> theirs...   **MONTESQUIEU 18**

Mesmerism is presently palmed off as leadership, even
though it is unrelated to thoughts developed and convictions
drawn independent of crowd pressure. Mirroring is not an easy
task (ask a politician). In a plural society, the common winds of
opinion change direction without advance notice. People-politi-
cian tactics lead to confusion and disaster. The crowd may change
its mind after election and the elected politician (never having
developed true leadership) becomes insecure or refines the talent

for deception. True leadership is built upon principle, not the impulsivity of diverse groups and mass persuasion. Crowd pleasing is devoid of independently derived intelligent thought and conviction. Politicians who primarily seek to please have abandoned their responsibility of contributing to the moral strength of our nation.

> A feature of leadership is to maintain high morale. There are two types of morale: 1) congeniality of groups, member to member and, 2) the group leader shows he is attaining what the group wants: morale of congeniality and morale of leadership. You lose some morale of congeniality in a plural society
> **(RAYMOND B. CATTELL**, *Personal Communication).*

An expanding and ever changing society requires different types of leaders. A desirable and rare leader is capable of negotiation without compromise of principle.

Every country has a unique history which offers significant input for the *modus operandi* of its leadership. In Japan, the foundation of leadership is derived from a stable and long history. The United States does not have this advantage, as it is a relatively new country. Whether or not American democracy survives depends on launching a thorough investigation of the role of leadership in other powerful nations. Today there is massive and concentrated industrial power in Japan and West Germany. We may be adding Korea, the Soviet Union and China in the near future. If the United States fails to carry out this research, we will find ourselves in the position of follower rather than leader in one area after another. For example, Japan set new standards in the automobile industry by manufacturing automobiles which could travel more miles per gallon of fuel long before Detroit took action by shifting gears and acknowledging the trend of the times. American automobile manufacturers are without excuse in claiming unpredictability of oil prices, which increased significantly beginning in 1974. Corporate America had become both fat and sleepy during the 1950's and 1960's.

Prescient leadership does not take good times for granted. We live in an extremely fast and changing world which means America must be vigilant and observe what is happening in other countries and be willing to adopt new measures when necessary. Only then can we be a leader in some areas and avoid lapsing into the stupor of conformity.

> In a study of small groups, we had ordinary leaders and technical leaders. For example, the State Department provides technical leaders who advise the president. There are leaders for a democracy and leaders for a dictatorship. Karl Marx would be a technical leader. He influenced people which resulted in pressure on the leader **(RAYMOND B. CATTELL,** *Personal Communication).*

America requires 1,000 uncompromising leaders (of diverse talents and experience), scattered throughout the nation, who exert relentless pressure upon elected politicians and officials by stressing the urgency of national interests without suppressing or seeking to destroy the progress of other nations. Without guidance and direction from leaders possessed of strong character and wisdom, our nation will continue to diminish toward a leaderless state of anarchy.

REFERENCES

1. Plato. Volume 7. Page 377.

2. Cattell, R.B. (1987). *Beyondism: religion from science.* New York: Praeger. Page 198.

3. Ibid. Page 214.

4. de Stael, Madame (1964). *On politics, literature and national character.* Garden City, NY: Doubleday. Page 89.

5. Evans, Bergen (1954). *The spoor of spooks and other nonsense.* Quoted in *The great quotations* (1960). Compiled by George Seldes. Lyle Stuart, NY: Caesar-Stuart. Page 247.

6. Aristotle (1977). *Great treasury of western thought.* Eds. Mortimer J. Adler and Charles Van Doren. New York and London: R.R. Bowker. Page 737.

7. Mill, J.S. (1970). *The subjection of women.* Cambridge and London: The M.I.T. Press. Page 23.

8. Cattell, R.B. and Child, D. (1975). *Motivation and dynamic structure.* New York: Wiley. Page 199.

9. Montesquieu. Volume 38. Page 16.

10. Russell, Bertrand. *Education.* Quoted in *Great treasury of western thought* (1977). Eds. Mortimer J. Adler & Charles Van Doren. New York and London: R.R. Bowker. Page 549.

11. Plato. Volume 7. Page 785.

12. Lao-Tse. Quoted in *The great quotations* (1960). Compiled by George Seldes. Lyle Stuart, NY: Caesar-Stuart Book. Page 398.

13. Cattell, R.B. (1972). *A new morality from science: Beyondism.* New York: Pergamon. Page 383.

14. Cattell, R.B. (1987). *Beyondism: religion from science.* New York: Praeger. Page 47.

15. Hegel. Volume 46. Page 141.

16. Cattell, R.B. (1987). *Beyondism: religion from science.* New York: Praeger. Page 222.

17. Tacitus. Volume 15. Page 204.

18. Montesquieu. Volume 38. Page 373.

CHAPTER SEVEN

INDIVIDUALISM vs. EQUALITY

Individualism as a concept rarely is understood, let alone appreciated (particularly since 1960). How do we define individuality? Individuality is commonly perceived as eccentricity—one who is different and strange. An assumption follows: we can not make sense of a certain individual, therefore s/he exhibits individuality. Worthy individuality includes autonomy, strength of character and personal values which evoke envy rather than disgust. As values change, our view of individualism changes. The key question pertaining to individuality revolves around how we differ from others, not whether we differ.

Ideologically speaking, individualism has been replaced by the desire for equality. Equality of dignity is a noble concept which we prefer not to discuss. Nearly everyone accepts equality of opportunity; almost no one thinks about equality of self-imposed dignity. Equality ignores and fails to reward differences of effort. How can there be equality of material goods when there will always be inequality of the willingness to work hard? Inequality in the desire to exert energy ought not be confused with inequality in the disposition to lie, distort and exploit others.

During the past thirty-five years, there has been more activity in the name of equal rights than during the preceding two centuries. The conflict pertains to equality of opportunity and unjust laws which provide inequitable advantages for those who are privileged. The legislation of equal rights in a democratic society creates a paradox. Totalitarian societies are geared to enforce "equality" by maintaining uniformly low living standards. Our concern is that present-day views of equality halt individual and national growth.

> In republican governments, men are all equal; equal they are also in despotic governments: in the former, because they are everything; in the latter, because they are nothing.   **MONTESQUIEU 1**

It is naive to think that constitutional rights create a great nation. America has excelled due to high individual and national cultural standards juxtaposed with constitutional rights. Historically speaking, the marriage of high standards and constitutional rights is unsurpassed. Divorce of this combination presently occurs in the wake of unprecedented erosion of former cultural standards. Just as constitutional rights are meaningless without high cultural standards (justice), equal rights are nonexistent without an emphasis on and manifestation of individuality. In fact, one thousand rights have no meaning without the dignity of ethical individuality.

A quick scan of the last two centuries shows unmistakably that the thinking and contributions of exceptional individuals evoked awe. We are the heirs and beneficiaries of former individual sacrifices. Conversely, power today resides in a group's ability to make noise, not in its contribution to present and future generations. The present undermining of noteworthy individuality requires examination.

> The deeper natures never forget themselves and never become anything else than what they were.
>   **KIERKEGAARD 2**

Crowds lacking the barest trace of individuality are impulsive, unpredictable and respond to appetite and selfish interest. Pavlov's dogs provide an accurate analogue in their salivating to the ringing of bells.

How did individualism acquire a bad name? The turning point can be traced to Hitler and World War II. Ever since Hitler, it is as if we have adopted antagonism to true individuality. One misguided leader promised his people paradise on earth and in return gave them war and death. Can one man permanently alter our historical respect for stalwart individuality? We can not progress in matters of equality with justice for all until we first resolve our confusion in matters pertaining to individuality. True equality issues from a foundation of respect for personal dignity. Character and personal dignity are the core of true individuality.

> Whatsoever has a potentiality must first have a character of its own; and its potentiality will consist in its having a reach beyond that character to some other.
>
> **PLOTINUS 3**

Remove the concept of dignity and we destroy any respectable discussion of individualism. It is true, admiration for worthwhile individuality is diminishing; only tough and uncompromising thinking will restore it to a resemblance of its former status. A major reason America has been "a country of countries" is that during our history, unrivaled emphasis was placed upon respectable selfhood. Can we remain a strong and influential nation without restoring the value of personal dignity and character?

> It is from the mind of the creative individual, reacting to the situations created by the group, that the group alone draws its capacity to live and grow. **R.B. CATTELL 4**

Denial of racial differences robs us of our individuality. The so-called liberal mind tends to minimize, if not eliminate, the fact of racial differences. This attitude evinces non-liberal and stingy thought processes. Appreciation for the dissimilarity of races is vital if democracy is to survive. Admitting to the existence of racial differences requires honesty and maturity. Pretending that differences do not exist (ignoring or denying the painfully obvious) is a sign of indifference or ignorance.

> ...without heredity there would simply not be an individual, for it both makes him and ensures his individuality.
>
> **R.B. CATTELL 5**

Equal rights is a complex notion; it also includes the right to be equally stupid and arrogant. Characteristic of our age are terms with more inherent pitfalls (in the present interpretations and implications) than practical benefits. Among these terms are the following buzzwords: freedom, rights, democracy and privilege. Historically, people viewed freedom from the perspective of responsibility, knowing full well the cost of maintaining high standards of freedom. What is freedom without responsibility? It is a strange concoction which demoralizes and encourages the degenerate side of life to dominate.

Equality is not as distasteful a notion as it is impractical. What will be the effects of enforcing equality by law over a period of one hundred years? Do employment quotas for minorities strengthen or lessen racial discrimination over a period of time?

Genetic reality discriminates. It is futile to imagine that thousands of years hence, all races will have merged to such extent that it will be impossible to distinguish racial traits. Wishful thinking of this order reveals underlying contempt and personal insecurity. Additionally, the hope that unrestricted mingling of the races will lead to the elimination of war is false. It is a delusion contradicted by the history of fratricidal strife—civil wars.

Our challenge is to seek out the strength of different races, without being blind to their shortcomings. Appreciation of the variation in racial cultures (and their contributions) constitutes a major part of enjoyment in life. Why be ashamed of whatever race we happen to be? To be ashamed of our race (or racial mixture) is a sign of individual ineptitude rather than racial inferiority. Superior and inferior are terms which our present culture prefers to ignore. Yet no passenger hesitates to prefer a superior pilot in the cockpit to a less experienced one, if s/he has the choice. Some people (in their distorted and abusive thinking) accept an inferior pilot in the cockpit as long as they are not a passenger on that jet. This kind of thinking must be abolished as it threatens the survival of humanity.

We can ill afford beliefs which result in racial stupor. Both extremes: 1) believing a particular race to be superior to all others and, 2) denying painfully obvious differences among races, qualify for the term "racial stupor."

The greatest racial prejudice of all times fails to appreciate racial differences. Consider the many advantages each race inherits based upon contributions of other races. Only ignoracists and ignoramuses desire racial equality. Racial equality is undesirable because it upsets evolution as argued in Beyondism. Without competition among races, sails hang limply, absent winds which activate the ship of life.

The belief in racial equality in deciding questions of

immigration is a possible cause of degeneration
(**RAYMOND B. CATTELL**, *Personal Communication*).

The presence of strength of character and dignity of selfhood greatly reduce racial hatred. Man-made laws can not diminish genetic truth of various races. Mature individuals acknowledge positive and negative characteristics of each race. As creatures of flesh and blood, no one escapes the positive and negative side of life. The genetic blending of distinct races (as a solution for today's problems) eliminates not only the shortcomings but also the strengths of different races.

The course of events determine racial suicide
(**RAYMOND B. CATTELL**, *Personal Communication*).

The collective strength of a race rises and falls in time (Greek, Roman, Mayan Indian, Spanish, French, British and German to cite examples). A strong individual (as a strong nation) strives in order to remain strong. Without continuous striving, the "strong" are in a position to fall fast and hard.

Future crises will loom much larger than racial ideology. Shortly, all races, particularly in cultures with cars, computers and chicanery, will be forced to come to grips with creating substance in life, substance in terms of worthwhile human interactions. Demand for quality life experience will be a greater issue than the color of our skin. Our challenge is to increase contributions of all races (made possible by acknowledging those positive qualities which distinguish one race from another). The elimination of racial hatred is a poor tradeoff when placed alongside the vast gains and contributions of each race. Notwithstanding, racial hatred is unacceptable at all times.

Is the idea of selection really unjust? Is it not justice? And is it not true that in ordinary life, selection plays a major part? Are not people selected for their particular jobs? **M. NICOLL 6**

A factor in the strength of America has been her high regard for genuine individuality. For example, a man was a man and a woman a woman—there was no foolish nonsense which asked, "What is a man?" and "What is a woman?" The intent of both of these questions is a claim that man and woman are indefinable and without differences. The identical thinking which ignores differences among races seeks to ignore differences between man and woman. It is the cutting edge which makes life worth living. Without a cutting edge, life is bland, insipid, uninspiring, burdensome, frivolous and lacking in taste. By cutting edge, we mean that which distinguishes us, not that which we have in common. The fact that we eat, sleep and drink is nothing to get excited about. There is no salvation based upon the common and inescapable necessities of life. Incontestably the sexes have much in common; can we learn to respect and appreciate our preferences and dislikes (which we do not have in common)?

True individuality occurs with the formation of identity. To downplay the development of noteworthy individuality is to deny identity-formation. Our present confusion and wandering cultural tastes make it difficult to define individualism.

> Great minds are sure to madness near aligned And thin partitions do their bounds divide (Dryden). This is a poet's statement of a common illusion because we know that creative individuals are less subject to psychosis
> **(RAYMOND B. CATTELL**, *Personal Communication).*

Dryden presumes that great minds (a clear indication of individuality) hover in proximity to madness. The following quote explicitly clarifies what individuality is not:

> If you have to maintain self-esteem by pulling down the standing of others, you are extraordinarily unfortunate in a variety of ways. Since you have to protect your feeling of personal worth by noting how unworthy everybody around you is, you are not provided with any data that are convincing evidence of your having personal worth; so it gradually evolves into "I am not as bad as the other swine." **H.S. SULLIVAN 7**

In America Ralph Waldo Emerson and Thoreau exemplified rugged individuality. Historically speaking, Epictetus, Socrates, Marcus Aurelius, Hypatia of Egypt, Savonarola of Florence, Descartes, Madame de Stael, Nietzsche, John Stuart Mill and presently, Gorbachev, Margaret Thatcher and Raymond B. Cattell exhibit the mental rigor requisite for high levels of individuality.

> As any change must begin somewhere, it is the single individual who will experience it and carry it through.
> **C. JUNG 8**

Equality removes the incentive for developing a cutting edge; fully implemented equality demoralizes. To achieve equality requires an environment that suppresses freedom; equality and freedom are incompatible. When cultural norms and laws fail to reward great personal sacrifices (most essential for making contributions of value for today as well as the future), what incentive will there be to choose the sober and relentlessly demanding path which leads to an evolving and substantive individual?

The notion of equality is popular in America. I attribute this to individuality being misrepresented as bizarre, inscrutable, unpalatable, deceptive and unaccountable; crowd mentality insists upon equality which obstructs the development of outstanding individuals by coercing people to move in a hapless and mediocre direction. The present cry for equal rights is a case in point: we are suspicious and weary of irresponsible and abusive application of freedom. Individuality and freedom are devoid of sustainable meaning when citizens claim the right to add their personal brand of selfishness to these historically honorable qualities. Freedom and individuality are interdependent; diminish one and we automatically restrict the other. With full equality, people do not choose; the major decisions have already been made.

> True, if quality of intellect could be made up for by quantity, it might be worthwhile to live even in the great world; but, unfortunately, a hundred fools together will not make one wise man. **SCHOPENHAUER 9**

Equality is specifically a euphemism which seeks to rectify gross injustices. Equality is an attempt to create justice but instead leads to injustice. Equal opportunity also means equal right to exploit (whether by citizens or by the government). This repulses for a very good reason: there can never be an equality of the ability and willingness to exploit as long as some people prefer honesty and goodness over and above evil.

> Man can live only with his own equals, and not even with these; for in the long run he cannot endure anyone's being his equal. **GOETHE 10**

We are barking up the wrong tree with equality as our goal. In practice, a society which insists on equality is as ineffective and deleterious as one which neuters all boys and girls. Who would choose that society?

> This is a prospect before which Nietzsche recoils. 'This degeneration and diminution of man,' he writes, 'into the dwarf animal of equal rights and claims, is possible, there is no doubt of it.' He views this possibility with 'an anxiety that is past all comparisons,' suggesting that one who recognizes its implications 'no longer knows any other nausea other than man—but perhaps also a new task!' And this task is that of prompting precisely the opposite sort of development... **R. SCHACHT 11**

Value in equality resides in equality of dignity for each human being. No one has an automatic right to dignity; everyone is challenged to develop personal dignity. Is there equality of honesty? There is equal opportunity for citizens to choose and develop the virtue of honesty. Imagine the folly in attempting to create laws which demand citizens to be equally honest (we can not promote honesty by approaching this virtue dishonestly). Dignity is a virtue which is self-created by hard work and integrity; dignity is not a constitutional right. We do not create dignity by passing a law which stipulates that all human beings be treated with equal dignity. Neither can we increase honesty by passing a law which demands honesty of all human beings. We must recognize and respect the limitations of law in regulating honesty and dignity. A law which states "every citizen has the right to be honest" is as misdirected as a philosophy which attempts to make sense of claims for equal rights. Everyone has the duty (not the right) to be honest and develop personal dignity.

Every time we insist on more equality, we do so at the cost of liberty and individuality. A mutual and culturally sanctioned understanding of individuality does not change its meaning with the onset of each decade. It is a privilege to introduce a forgotten standard of equality, one which dates back to 1800:

> There is, indeed, an innate equality belonging to every man which consists in his right to be independent of being bound by others to anything more than that to which he may also reciprocally bind them. **KANT 12**

All notions of equality which fail to include respect for true individuality, become slavery in time. We mistakenly think we are reducing injustice, or slavery, by promoting equality, but, instead, end up promoting slavery.

Equality of opportunity and equal rights as ideals ignore a constant truism: never will there be an equality of self-sacrifice. It is impossible to attain equality of the following altruistic virtues: the giving of time, caring, understanding and true compassion.

Since about 1960 an attitude has spread: keep your mouth shut, do not volunteer more information than necessary, cash the check and refrain from asking questions, look out for number one while pretending others do not exist and take as much as possible only to give the minimal return, if any return at all. America as an historical phenomenon is a luxury which took three centuries to create, and which we risk squandering within the next thirty years. The strength of our nation did not originate with equal rights and equal opportunity (as most people interpret these concepts). America was created on a foundation which set forth citizens' right to life, liberty and the pursuit of happiness. Pursuit meant the freedom to work hard, the freedom to tell the truth, the freedom to require mutuality without coercion and deception, the freedom to inspire people and the freedom to find inspiration. When a nation of citizens in one voice clamors for equal rights, that nation bears witness to an unprecedented waste of time, mind and energy.

> To have no interest except in one's formal right may be pure obstinacy, often a fitting accompaniment of a cold heart and restricted sympathies. It is uncultured people who insist most on their rights, while noble minds look on other aspects of the thing. **HEGEL 13**

America is in the process of abandoning the thinking and behavior which produced Abraham Lincoln. We wonder why there are no Abraham Lincolns today. Some individuals claim Lincolns exist in today's America. Lincolns are not created in environments which flood the mind with notions of equal rights.

The initial idea of equality is noble and idealistic; it appears to make the unable able and places limits upon those who thrive upon injustice. The idea is quite acceptable until mediocrity becomes the cherished standard. Strict adherence to laws of equality results in citizens who think alike and when collective thoughts lack in substance, we end with equality of nonsense: a state of mind whereby confusion eliminates the ability to exercise discernment. Equality never did and never will promote individuality.

> Does not our love of liberty, which seems to be inherent
> in all of us, rest squarely upon our inequalities?
> **R.J. WILLIAMS 14**

Irrespective of how we rationalize equality, contradictory notions can not support one another. If we lack the requisite intelligence for understanding this matter, may our intuitive integrity provide assistance. We must rediscover wisdom of the ages if we are to return to the status of a great nation. The creation of a great America was not an accident; by the year 2100 A.D., if we fail to bring about renewal through reversal of the present downward spiral of trends, America will have been an accident (when viewed through the corridors of time and history). Our country built a great tradition based on imperfect but at least water-tight principles.

> ...if I had a cask which is water-tight, and you one with
> a hole in it, and you should come and deposit with me
> your wine that I might put it into my cask, and then
> should complain that I also did not intrust my wine to
> you, for you have a cask with a hole in it. How then is
> there any equality here?   **EPICTETUS 15**

Libertarianism is a philosophy committed to individual rights. The central idea of libertarianism defends the right of each individual to choose how to live his/her life (without coercing or restricting others from living according to their choices). In a country which once had millions of acres to be pioneered, with the majority of citizens striving to increase self-reliance, integrity, a deep love of country for the right reasons and possessed with an attitude which sought to improve the quality of life for others, libertarianism as a philosophy contributed to the evolution of cultural standards. A firm commitment to libertarian philosophy (in its present interpretation and usage) is full of pitfalls and unresolvable contradictions.

> Individual rational discipline will be an adequate guar-
> antee of individual freedom only if and when society at
> large becomes a community of rational men [and women].
> **R.G. OLSON 16**

Libertarianism is a viable philosophy in a milieu of high

standards where citizens make constructive, as opposed to destructive, choices. A liberal position grants individuals the "freedom" or the "right" to live irresponsibly; but . . . who can possibly do this for any length of time without infringing upon the resources of society, the energy and time of fellow citizens? America's challenge (contingent to a sound libertarian philosophy) is to separate vicious misfits (who persistently wreck and destroy opportunities for self-improvement), from the truly abused, underprivileged and unfortunates. Secondly, how do we best help the helpless innocents without increasing the ranks of aimless and dejected individuals?

Sustainable freedom can not be separated from the promotion of virtue. All freedom which does not result in or lead to virtue is illusory.

> A society without a sense of its own fundamental moral principles is one in which the members of that society are not able to perceive clearly the worthiness of their actions. **DOUGLAS DEN UYL 17**

Thoughts about freedom, rights, democracy, equality and success are in a state of confusion due to the lack of consistent guiding principles. The right to choose how to live as long as we do not infringe upon the right of others to do the same, is impossible without standards of neighborly concern in thought and behavior. We can not have an attractive society which fails to set standards limiting destructive behavior, both to self and others. Who decides those levels? Previously, a high cultural standard provided a guiding influence. Citizens guided by principle and backbone decide when depravity infringes upon everyone's freedom.

Libertarians worry that government constantly interferes with our lives. We are concerned that life will become so equalized that the privilege of living will be debatable. A Jeffersonian adage states: they govern best who govern least. Bureaucracy expands in the attempt to sustain the whims of everyone's personal choices. Personal choices are necessary and useful when based upon a standard; without a standard, one brand of foolishness is indistinguishable from another.

Some interpret individuality as selfishness; throughout this chapter, we are referring to ethical individuality. Ethical individuality insists upon well-being rather than degeneracy. A century ago the trademark of individuality entailed sharing based upon the strength of self-reliance, not self-aggrandizement based upon abdication of responsibility. A network bonded citizens in the development and support of community. Ethical individualism respects the right to pursue happiness (which does not include the right to happiness). No human being is obligated to make us happy. We do not inherit happiness; everyone should be given an opportunity to learn what constitutes happiness.

Now more than ever, the survival of America and the preservation of freedom depend upon comprehensive and tough thinking followed by decisive action.

> ...it is also possible that hard imaginative thinking has not increased so as to keep pace with the expansion and complication of human societies and organizations. That is the darkest shadow upon the hopes of mankind.
>
> **H.G. WELLS 18**

Efforts aimed at equality which simultaneously undermine the value of character development are ill-advised. Those who look to government to solve problems believe there is salvation in money. Money is a temporary solution; character is fueled on its own merits and is transferable to the next generation. Aristotle said that it is not wealth but character that lasts. Government can help, but help is inevitably of short-term value until we as citizens acquire the fortitude to investigate our backyards and resolve to restore principles of character based upon ethical individualism rather than loose libertarian thinking.

H.G. Wells was no small prophet. He was disheartened by the state of thinking modern man had acquired at the end of World War II. He believed the world to be at a major turning point best depicted as a shift from the rational to the irrational. Life would be liquidated. The present would fail to leave a trace or pattern which explained thoughts and actions. This means it is impossible to predict the near future. Certainly this is true in a world of constant economic fluctuation.

Not only do we despise history in our present state of mind, we are hopelessly addicted to distraction and destructive habits. Our predilection avoids investigating the past, present and future.

> He would rather our species ended its story in dignity, kindliness and generosity, and not like drunken cowards in a daze or poisoned rats in a sack.**H.G. WELLS 19**

America is at a critical intersection, every bit as critical as the Civil War. Major and rapid changes in the world present a daily challenge to our survival. Either we forge ahead or be forced into obscurity. We can ill afford the kind of equality which erodes those qualities which built a great nation. By downplaying the role of the individual, there no longer will be enough topsoil to nurture the growth and development of a crop worthy of harvest.

> The Renaissance began with the vigorous affirmation of man's creative individuality; it ended with a denial of it.
> **W.R. INGE 20**

REFERENCES

1. Montesquieu. Volume 38. Page 34.

2. Kierkegaard, S. (1941). *Fear and trembling.* Princeton, NJ: Princeton University Press. Page 61.

3. Plotinus. Volume 17. Page 58.

4. Cattell, R.B. (1972). *A new morality from science: Beyondism.* New York: Pergamon. Page 166.

5. Ibid. Page 260.

6. Nicoll, M. (1950). *The new man.* London: Vincent Stuart. Page 142.

7. Sullivan, H.S. (1953). *The interpersonal theory of psychiatry.* New York: Norton. Page 242.

8. Jung, C. (1964). *Man and his symbols*. Garden City, NY: Doubleday. Page 101.

9. Schopenhauer, A. (1901). *The wisdom of life*. New York and London: M.Walter Dunne. Page 19.

10. Goethe, J.W. von (1659). *Goethe's Poetische Werke*: Vol. 2. von Maximen u. Reflexionen #1405. Stuttgart: J.G. Cotta'sche.*

11. Schacht, R. (1983). *Nietzsche*. London: Routledge & Kegan Paul. Page 385.

12. Kant. Volume 42. Page 401.

13. Hegel. Volume 46. Page 120.

14. Williams, R.J. (1953). *Free and unequal*. Austin: University of Texas Press. Page 5.

15. Epictetus. Volume 12. Page 244.

16. Olson, R.G. (1965). *Morality of self-interest*. New York: Harcourt, Brace & World. Page 154.

17. Machan, T.R. (ed.) (1982). *The libertarian reader*. Quote is from chapter: "Freedom and virtue" by Douglas Den Uyl. Totowa, NJ: Rowman—division of Littlefield & Adams. Page 213.

18. Wells, H.G. (1968). *The last books of H.G. Wells: the happy turning and mind at the end of its tether*. London: H.G. Wells Society. Page 64.

19. Ibid.

20. Inge, W.R. (1948). *The end of an age*. London: Putnam. Page 22.

*Note: On reference #10, the German (original source) follows: "Der Mensch kann nur mit seinesgleichen leben und auch mit denen nicht; denn er kann auf die Lange nicht leiden, dass ihm jemand gleich sei."

CHAPTER EIGHT

LOVE vs. NARCISSISM

Everyone wants to be loved, but only a few people effectively share genuine love. How has this state of affairs come about? Since 1960, proof of love has been often entangled with hate. We claim true love with the presence of hatred. Could it be that the love-hate ratio is shifting in a negative direction? Millions resist "love" in order to avoid the wolf of hatred. Sigmund Freud first popularized awareness of the relationship between love and hate. The average person is unaware of a most important aspect for understanding love and hate—ambivalence.

> ...by this [ambivalence] we mean a directing of antithetical feelings (affectionate and hostile) towards the same person. **FREUD 1**

> ...ambivalence...the consequence once more of one of the universal characteristics of infantile sexuality. **FREUD 2**

> Normal adults do, undoubtedly, succeed in separating these two attitudes, and do not find themselves compelled to hate their love-objects and love as well as hate their enemies. But this seems to be the result of later development. In the first phases of the love-life ambivalence is evidently the rule. Many people retain this archaic trait throughout life... **FREUD 3**

It is important to recognize the significance of the term "archaic." During childhood, ambivalence is unavoidable as part

of the cost of learning to love. Mature love diminishes ambivalence. Irrespective of age, a strong presence of ambivalence
indicates infantile sexuality. Love occurs when the lover is not
under compulsion to provide evidence of love through occasional
manifestation of hatred. Our generation is skeptical in matters
pertaining to love and for a good reason: the condition of arrested
development and immaturity is not conducive to the experience
of fulfilling love.

Millions of citizens could confess sexual promiscuity (if not
presently, certainly in the past). Did we learn anything from
experimenting sexually or did our experiences doom many of us
to a lifetime of hopeless infantile egocentricity, loneliness and
bitterness?

The foremost consideration of this chapter belongs to the
younger generation. They are the heirs of a hodgepodge of
contradictory ideas about sex and love. Most adults have problems of their own which get in the way of remembering the
challenge of romance when they were young adults. How is it
possible for us to be participants in matters of love when we have
little conception of what to aim for? Where do we begin?

> What we must be concerned with is concepts and atti-
> tudes to love and procreation in human life. In these
> must be included, for the whole truth, an adequate
> appreciation of the creativity of love and the importance
> of the mother-child relationship, in human society. To
> deny this may involve both an inability to accept reality,
> and this may have its roots in the fear of or denial of
> woman [femininity]. **DAVID HOLBROOK** 4

Fear of or denial of femininity is not restricted to males;
some females resist valuing that which is unique to femininity. A
successful male-female relationship is noted on the basis of its
balance. Males ought not be threatened by their passive or
feminine attitude. Females relinquish part of their wish for
masculinity for the purpose of developing femininity.

> These two themes are connected with the difference be-
> tween the sexes: one is characteristic of men and the
> other equally characteristic of women. In spite of the
> difference in their content there is an obvious correspon-
> dence between the two. Some factor common to both
> sexes is forced, by the difference between them, to
> express itself differently in the one and in the other...I

think that from the first, 'repudiation of femininity' would have been the correct description of this remarkable feature in the psychical life of mankind. **FREUD 5**

Nothing is negative or wrong in being a masculine female or a feminine male; there is ample conflict in a female whose masculinity overpowers her femininity and a male whose femininity dominates his masculinity. Precisely what is amiss? Both are out of balance. What does this have to do with love?

Love between man and woman is the cornerstone of our civilization. Eliminate this love and watch civilization disappear. Nations remain strong and stable as long as a solid family structure prevails.

What interferes with the development of love? Typical romance encompasses a world of cheats (those who engage sexually without loving) who have no desire or intention to develop love. This leads to intensified sexual irresponsibility, desperate sensuality and an overflowing obsession with sex. More than a few believe love is the pleasure of possessing somebody and somebody wanting to be possessed. Sometimes "love" is nothing more than mutual narcissism. Love can not thrive in an environment which encourages deficiency. What people call love is in many instances fear, sentiment, duty, obligation, dependency, or the need to control or be controlled.

Passion and sensuality are dimensions which complicate the development of love. Unfortunately, passion often manifests in two forms: 1) longing for affirmation, or 2) reliance upon fantasy. Sensual individuals have a major challenge: developing and maintaining tenderness coupled with sensuality. Unfocused sensuality leads to a vicious cycle of stimulation and anesthetization—ambivalence.

In only very few people of culture are the two strains of tenderness and sensuality duly fused into one...
FREUD 6

...there is something, I think, in true tenderness bewitching; few women ever meet it in men, and fewer still know how to value it when they do. **H. FIELDING 7**

Yes, sensuality is important, but . . . sensuality without tenderness is deadly.

Every individual faces the challenge of developing the ability to love. One of the many obstructions to love begins with excessive materialized mothering and materialized fathering (the demand for material goods as proof of another's love). These individuals have insatiable egos; only a similar individual could tolerate and endure living under such an arrangement.

Having explored the negative and unhealthy side of love, what constitutes progressive and healthy love? Albert Schweitzer believed that the essence of love is reverence for life.

LOVE IS . . .
1) inextricably connected with goodness.
2) mutually strengthening and inspires participants in the direction of maturity.
3) affection for each other's character.
4) commitment to caring, sharing, respect and growth.
5) wise and noble.
6) cherished by honest and worthy persons.
7) lovableness . . . if we fail to genuinely love ourselves, how can we expect others to love us?
8) self-cultivation and self-transformation.

A test for love follows: would we recommend our present situation to our brother, sister, son or daughter and have them call it love?

Sexuality is confused with the term "love." An ill-fated relationship can not separate affection from sexual experience. Particularly as adults, we withhold affection due to a popular notion that affection is an invitation to share bodies. This functions as a barrier to our experience of love. In our failure to demonstrate social maturity, small wonder we are a nation of sexually frustrated individuals. Sex and love are related; they are not inextricably bound to one another.

Nearly every human being enters adulthood with a pattern of limitations which prevent her/him from loving and being loved. The best indicators for loving and being loved is whether or not we separate ourselves from conditions which prevent love or, continue to construct additional obstacles which block the experience of love. Love is never mocked. Promiscuous sexual behavior provides evidence for the lack of substantial and deep love.

From 1960 onward, virginity has been viewed with embarrassment. What began as a bush-fire ended in a conflagration which consumed nearly everybody's virginity by the age of twenty, from coast to coast. A new awareness will arise which finds value in virginity. Secure males and females will have the privilege of loving with an unadulterated mind and a whole heart. Quality of sexual experience supersedes mere quantity of sexual experience. Consider the impact in a society whereby only fifty percent of twenty year olds are no longer virgins versus ninety percent of twenty year olds.

The sexual revolution of the latter part of this century did wonders to eradicate the kind of neurosis (sexual paralysis) extant at the end of the nineteenth century. The selfsame revolution simultaneously undermined love in the wake of social and sexual irresponsibility. Romance suffers grievously when personal ethics are wanting.

Can "love" be understood? Is it possible to elucidate a meaningful understanding of "love?" Before endeavoring to do so, we ought to divorce ourselves from much we have heard about love. The term "love" has been used in such varied contexts that it often ends up being nebulous. For example, it describes both compassion and sexuality. Take a moment and define love for yourself by pondering and writing what love means to you. It is one thing to enumerate examples of love; it is another to recognize the absence of love in the face of protestations to the contrary.

Kierkegaard (1843) believed,

"...no generation has learned from another to love..." 8

This idea may lack support, nonetheless, it is worthy of consideration.

In writing about love, we are not speaking about the love of God, or the scriptural definition that states: "God is love." How can we love God when we have difficulty loving our brother, spouse or country? How can we love another individual when we possess a foggy, contradictory view of love?

Spiritual love is preceded by the development of other abilities to love. We ought to make sure that the love we proclaim for God is not merely a substitute for our neglect of loving human beings. This admonition is not meant to devalue spiritual love; spiritual love even has the value of respect for morality.

Loving a dog or cat should not substitute for loving people. Loving a pet can lead to loving a human being. Regrettably, pets now receive more love than human beings give to one another.

During the early stages of life it is natural to be entirely self-centered. This self-involvement is summarized as, "I am the center of the universe; all that exists is for me and me alone." During this period of development we are sentience unlimited.

An oceanic feeling pervades our being as one sensation merges with another. Conversely, as adults this level of self-involvement is called narcissism. Narcissism is characterized by self-indulgence, presumption, pomposity, self-worship and egotism. By way of contrast, self-love develops identity. Self-love is necessary and healthy in a hostile world. Self-centeredness is narcissism and this arrangement of self-involvement is ironically, negation of the self. When narcissistic individuals are not the center of attention, they experience absence of self. A narcissistic individual experiences disequalibrium when: 1) unattended by others or, 2) preoccupied by a persistent need for distraction.

Affirmation of identity fulfills three objectives:
1) I exist and am distinct from all others.
2) I am lovable because I love.
3) The intuitive realization that inner development precedes the ability to love another human being.

Number three above is in reference to self-validation. A narcissistic individual can not self-validate due to arrested emotional development. This arrest is characterized as follows:

> ...only a poor devil, one of those who never have any luck; perhaps he was too poorly gifted, too ineffective to make a living, and belonged to that well-known type, the 'eternal suckling'—to those who are unable to tear themselves away from the joyous haven at the mother's breast, who hold fast all through their lives to their claim to be nourished by someone else.   **FREUD 9**

Self-love includes emotional maturity. Unstable, conflicting and unpredictable emotional experiences occur either with exclusive dependence on others or isolation, but not through interdependence.

An understanding of narcissism is indispensable for comprehending the meaning of enduring love. Particularly within the sphere of love lies great opportunity for self-deception. We may be sincerely convinced that we are in love whereas in reality, we are merely exalting self-indulgence.

> Therefore those who love for the sake of utility love for the sake of what is good for <u>themselves</u>, and those who love for the sake of pleasure do so for the sake of what is

> pleasant to <u>themselves</u>, and not in so far as the other is
> the person loved but in so far as he is useful or pleasant.
> **ARISTOTLE 10**

What is wrong with self-indulgence, notably when we are not hurting anybody? Plenty. Self-indulgence is to our hearts and minds as restricted breathing is to our lungs. As in a "mutual admiration society," narcissism constricts the self-realization of all participants. The more prevalent the narcissism, the less shared participation. Are we not all self-indulgent? We are but not to the degree of excluding instead of relating with people.

> For the child loves himself first and only later learns to
> love others, and to sacrifice something of his own ego to
> them.   **FREUD 11**

As an adult, it is only in loving others that we continue to be loved. Negation of ourselves (as in narcissism), prevents the partaking of love from others. Electric current does not flow where it can not be received.

Emotional interdependence and mutual love keep us from withering away in psychological sickness and physiological disease. Love is an active energy, essential to health and well-being. It is not a luxury reserved for the lucky and created by accident.

> <u>Love</u> is a matter of <u>feeling</u>, not of will or volition, and I
> cannot love because I <u>will</u> to do so, still less because I
> <u>ought</u> (I cannot be necessitated to love); hence there is no
> such thing as a <u>duty to love</u>.   **KANT 12**

This view of love refers to the adult world. In part, children learn to love as they are directed. Stated more succinctly, we cannot love simply because we want to, even less because we ought to. Duty is to love as force is to choice. The greater the coercion the less choice.

We can be taught to forsake a portion of self-involvement and thereby increase our experience of involvement with others. Through mutual identification with other's feelings, through honesty, by sincerely caring for the welfare of others, bearing our partner's consequential interests in mind (through these and more), love begins to manifest.

Of the classics, Pascal's observation on love is particularly discerning:

> Hence one is inclined to love him who makes us feel it, for he has not shown us his own riches, but ours.
>
> PASCAL 13

Love calls forth the best qualities rather than a magnificent projection of ourselves.

It is a blow to our ego to be unable to command love, yet this very injury to the ego precedes the ability to reciprocate love.

> It seems that an accumulation of narcissistic libido over and above a certain level becomes intolerable. We might well imagine that it was this that first led to the investment of objects, that the ego was obliged to send forth its libido in order not to fall ill of an excessive accumulation of it.
>
> FREUD 14

Freud did not limit the term "libido" to sexual instinct; it also encompasses the ability to love. Either we develop the ability to love or we increase mental disturbance.

A highly narcissistic individual can not wrest free from Milton's "perpetual childhood of prescription." During early development, each new-born child introjects parental prescriptions. Prescriptions provide the child with support and structure necessary for development. Parental narcissism is the exclusive reflection of the parental self in the child. Since the child inherits genes from both parents, s/he automatically reflects some of their characteristics. Offspring, drawing genes from their "pool of genetic possibility," have infinite potential for creating their specific individuality and identity.

It is important to distinguish between parental love and parental narcissism. Parental narcissism operates when the parent insists that offspring <u>exclusively</u> <u>reflect</u> their thoughts, values, feelings and patterns of behavior. Parental love recognizes the uniqueness in a new-born child and serves to prime the child's pump by providing access to his or her well of living waters. Parental narcissism rejects divergence from parental reflection and demands conformity.

Personal identity is made possible by connecting with our genetic well of living waters. Narcissistic parents resist identity-formation in their children. As narcissism commands movement in one direction only (self-indulgence), it can not tolerate identity-formation in the child. Identity is formed by observing and adopting similarity (traits relevant to one's self) and recognizing dissimilarity in all human beings. The key element is interrelationship. Narcissism interferes with identity-formation by failing to incorporate from others—something in addition to ourselves. "Others" are debased to a mere means to an end—the narcissist's ends of self-gratification.

> Societies have so far found little defense against this dependent tapeworm behavior since narcism is by its nature a skilled and obstinate passive defense against within-group moral demands.**RAYMOND B. CATTELL** 15

The perpetual demand for attention prevents identity-formation. Without identity it is impossible to love with constancy. Narcissism seeks its own reflection—more of the same.

Kant informs us, "But what is done from constraint is not done from love." 16 Narcissism constrains in a closed system whereas love expands in an open system. Narcissism is a dead-end road; love connects the roadways of the universe.

Either we love or experience the torment of being unable to love.

> Fathers and teachers, I ponder, 'What is hell?' I maintain that it is the suffering of being no longer able to love.
> **DOSTOEVSKY** 17

Freud informs us that a narcissist's only sexual object is his own ego. This observation illustrates the hell and arrest of confinement within our ego. A prisoner's attempt to escape from a penitentiary presents as great a challenge as a narcissist's difficulty in springing free from the vise of ego. In varying degrees, we all are challenged with sacrificing narcissism to qualify and participate in the experience of love.

> ...only extraordinary persons of great gift are immune from narcism. **E. FROMM** 18

> A healthy love of oneself is essential to the development of self-respect and self-confidence; excessive narcism takes the form of loving oneself to the exclusion of others, of losing sight of the fact that others are sentient beings, that others, too, are constituting egos, each constructing and experiencing a unique world. In short, narcists are solipsists who experience the world and other individuals as existing solely for them. **I. YALOM** 19

Inherent in parental narcissism are grave misunderstandings. Adult narcissists tend to blame their parents for whatever ills befall them. Narcissism can be acquired by example and many adult narcissists learned it from their narcissistic parents. Once conscious of the rigid and narrow limits of narcissism, forgiveness of narcissistic parents is desirable. Continuing to blame one's parents guarantees no hope or cure from narcissistic sickness. Forgiving means freeing ourselves from the prison of repetition, rage, taking others hostage and the perpetuation of emotional abuse.

The challenge for those who find themselves with narcissistic individuals is to assist in transforming the narcissist's energy in a mutually beneficial direction. The consciousness of a narcissist requires elevation beyond the one-way street which clamors for constant attention. Only a saint or a masochist can possibly bear up under limitless narcissistic demands.

Having identified the detrimental side of narcissism, there is a positive side:

> The positive role of narcissism is illustrated by the fact that leading doctors and artists measure high on narcissism. This indicates that narcissism has a function in society (**RAYMOND B. CATTELL**, *Personal Communication*).

Clearly, love is an expansive and dynamic energy. Love can not survive with the boredom of restrictive repetition; rather she embraces the universe. Love does not yield to our will, neither is she a commodity to be exchanged. Love lives when shared.

> Universal love is not only psychologically possible; it is the only complete and final way in which we are able to love. **TEILHARD DE CHARDIN** 20

An understanding of love is made possible by unveiling the tunnels of narcissism. Narcissism begins and ends with ourselves. Love begins with others, moves through us back to others and repeats this movement ad infinitum throughout the universe. Narcissism holds us hostage and seeks to take others hostage. Narcissism in the simplest of language is self-indulgence. Love insists on breathing whereas narcissism stifles and suffocates individual development (especially within the context of a relationship).

True love leads not only to the best present (by calling forth our highest potential), but simultaneously champions the finest future. In order for love to flourish we must reduce our individual narcissism and arrest the currently popular trend which undermines the feminine principle.

REFERENCES

1. Freud, S. (1920, 1935). *A general introduction to psychoanalysis.* Trans. by Joan Riviere. New York: Liveright. Page 370.

2. Freud, S. (1959). *Collected papers.* New York: Basic Books. Volume V, Page 263.

3. Ibid. Page 263.

4. Holbrook, D. (1964). *The quest for love.* London: Methuen. Page 203.

5. Freud, S. (1959). *Collected papers.* New York: Basic Books. Volume V, Pages 354-355.

6. Ibid. Volume IV. Page 211.

7. Fielding. Volume 37. Page 355.

8. Kierkegaard, S. (1941). *Fear and trembling.* Princeton, NJ: Princeton University Press. Page 190.

9. Freud, S. (1959). *Collected papers.* New York: Basic Books. Volume IV, Page 471.

10. Aristotle. Volume 9. Page 407.

11. Freud, S. (1920, 1935). *A general introduction to psychoanalysis.* Trans. by Joan Riviere. NY: Liveright. Page 181.

12. Kant. Volume 42. Page 375.

13. Pascal. Volume 33. Page 174.

14. Freud, S. (1920, 1935). *A general introduction to psychoanalysis.* Trans. by Joan Riviere. New York: Liveright. Pages 364-365.

15. Cattell, R.B. (1972). *A new morality from science: Beyondism.* New York: Pergamon. Page 247.

16. Kant. Volume 42. Page 376.

17. Dostoevsky, F. (1933, 1949). *The brothers karamazov.* New York: The Heritage Press. Page 247.

18. Fromm, E. (1980). *Greatness and limitations of Freud's thoughts.* New York: Harper & Row. Page 13.

19. Yalom, I. (1985). *The theory and practice of group psychotherapy.* New York: Basic Books. Page 402.

20. Teilhard de Chardin, P. (1972). *On love.* New York: Harper & Row. Page 90.

CHAPTER NINE

EXCELLENCE vs. MEDIOCRITY

A s the twentieth century draws to a close, America faces her greatest challenge. Citizens of Japan, West Germany and Korea are bound to produce excellence or find themselves doomed to mediocrity. America became a great country because many citizens possessed characteristics which built a strong foundation. A citizen stood out from the crowd by virtue of manifesting qualities admired by everyone. Conversely, today's citizen stands out on the basis of either possessing a singular talent or simply by being strange. Much that is esteemed today will be of limited value fifty years hence (either practically or conceptually) and qualifies for the description of mediocre, or worse, bizarre.

Standards for mass acclaim have changed since the time of Ralph Waldo Emerson. Character in Emerson's time was the first prerequisite for respect from others; today a rock singer and a football player receive public applause without inquiry into their character and real contributions.

> There is a recognition by philosophers that in order for everybody to have freedom, each must sacrifice some of their own, e.g., you can't commit murder when you feel like it. In more subtle ways, the fact of paying taxes is widespread
> (**RAYMOND B. CATTELL**, *Personal Communication*).

One hundred years ago our cultural standard ignored or

ostracized bizarre behavior. Today strange behavior is misconstrued as individuality. The issue at stake: upon what basis do
we qualify for individuality and excellence? Freedom exists to the
degree personal and national ethics prevail.

The Eastern World continues to stifle social individuality.
Nonetheless, governments of leading Eastern countries place a
premium on academic excellence and all other contributions
which make a country strong. Sacrifice and dedication are the
order of the day for citizens. You are an individual in the East to
the extent that your contribution promotes your country among
other countries. National and racial pride play a significant role
in the collective effort of Eastern countries such as Japan, Korea
and China.

> True human progress—progress in inborn powers—has
> been ensured largely by the continual competition of
> racial groups.   **R.B. CATTELL 1**

Democracy as practiced by millions of Americans has never
existed on a large scale. It allows citizens the luxury and freedom
to pursue happiness in their own way. No one relinquishes
freedom without a fight. Too often, freedom is identified as the
right to obnoxious selfishness. A permissive and indulgent
society does not defend true freedom (freedom with attendant
responsibilities), but exerts great energy to overcome obstacles to
a proclaimed "right" of exploitation. Freedom has come to include
so many possibilities that its meaning suffers. The best definition
for present-day American freedom parallels the thinking of the
people who lived at the time of the Tower of Babel:

> ...now nothing will be restrained from them, which they
> have imagined to do.   **(Genesis 11:6) 2**

There is a difference between extreme lack of restraint in a
society's citizens and a society which cultivates originality.

When a country is painfully conservative, e.g. America until
1960, a certain number of bizarre people add value—they unnerve
the smugness of conservatism. Remove standards of personal
excellence (apart from IQ, banking accounts and noble birth),
increase the desire for isolation and no country can defend itself.
We believe in a strong defense; the greatest defense is a citizenry
united in personal excellence. Each citizen is a guardian of
society. When we fail to fulfill minimal guardianship, anything

can happen. Rampant odd behavior makes a travesty of freedom. What constitutes odd behavior? Having to ask the question shows we have exceeded an acceptable level of such behavior.

Excellence is not a thing apart from proper application of money, intelligence, good fortune and authority. Descartes makes our point:

> For to be possessed of good mental powers is not suffi-
> cient; the principal matter is to apply them well. The
> greatest minds are capable of the greatest vices as well
> as of the greatest virtues...   **DESCARTES 3**

One notion is that it does not matter how we get to the top so long as we get there. Eliminate the future after our death and we almost could be persuaded to adopt the preceding presumption. Judgment, supported by the Law of the Universe, takeš place continuously, independent of our awareness and without direct intervention from God.

> ...everything follows from the necessity of the divine
> nature, and comes to pass according to the eternal laws
> and rules of nature...   **SPINOZA 4**

Untutored minds ascribe incidentals to the intervention of God. Many individuals who believe in God in truth exhibit belief in personal vanity.

Three years ago Joe desired a kidney transplant hoping to no longer require the use of a dialysis machine. Every day Joe waited for a phone call. One evening the telephone rang. Immediately, his missionary sister proclaimed, "God is good, God has blessed and Praise the Lord." Joe received the kidney transplant. He was informed that the kidney had belonged to a young jogger who ran a stop sign and was killed instantly. Joe's brother astutely put the question, "was God good to the jogger?" Joe's body rejected the transplant and he nearly died during six miserable weeks and three operations (kidney transplant, exploratory and rejection of the kidney). As if Joe had not experienced enough torture, as a consequence of the operations he now requires three four-hour sessions of dialysis per week instead of the former two. After completion of the operations, Joe's surgeon asked, "are you still my friend?"

Does the preceding story reduce or eliminate our need to believe in God? Of course not. It does ask that we mature and exercise restraint in ascribing events to God. The purpose of devotion to God is not to save our skin. Millions waste a lifetime anxiously wondering whether they will go to heaven or to some other place. This anxiety is misplaced energy which does not lead to an honest, purposeful and upright life (of value to ourselves and to the community). Many religious individuals show disrespect to God. Affectation of piety is a poor touchstone for determining sincerity and devotion in spiritual matters.

> Much courage to be, created by religion, is nothing else than the desire to limit one's own being and to strengthen this limitation through the power of religion. And even if religion does not lead to or does not directly support pathological self-reduction, it can reduce the openness of man to reality which is himself. In this way religion can protect and feed a potentially neurotic state.
>
> **PAUL TILLICH 5**

The purpose of religion is to elevate our lives to a higher consciousness; it can also keep us superstitious. Without excellence, spiritual experience is a one-way ticket to mediocrity. Excellence in spirituality requires unselfish sincerity.

Mediocrity is the offspring of egalitarian ideology. There are two kinds of egalitarian: 1) the right to equal opportunity (as in the constitution), and 2) a belief that people are actually born equal in ability. America is rapidly moving in the direction of an egalitarian nation, shifting gears circa 1960. A case in point for the second type would be the refusal to permit examinations during the 1960's which would have pointed out great differences among individuals. There is a law: as egalitarian aspirations are enforced, individual striving and group excellence disappear.

Two centuries ago, Hegel wrote The Philosophy of History . This work clearly demonstrates that many centuries contributed to American freedom. Our freedom did not begin in 1620 or 1776. The thoughts developed during the ancient Greek Empire led to our experience of freedom. We must open our eyes and not take lightly the challenge of preserving freedom.

Following are four categories which demonstrate hypothetical demographic population changes in the context of an increasing egalitarian philosophy. My own estimates indicate the following trends:

	1776 to 1960	1960 to Present
Individuality	12%	3%
Weirdness	3%	12%
Excellence	60%	25%
Mediocrity	25%	60%

> The more perfect egalitarian democracy becomes, the more naturally its citizens resemble each other, the more they will all freely desire the same things. Diversity would gradually be banished from such a society, not by censure but by general disapproval or mere indifference. The majority's omnipotence would eliminate even the urge to stray from prevailing opinions. Original minds that work against the popular grain would gradually wither—those, that is, that were not stillborn—not because of persecution, but simply for lack of an audience, for lack of anyone to contradict them.
> **J.F. REVEL 6**

True excellence is not grafted; it is a tree whose roots and branches are inseparable. One of the great deceptions of our age is the unchallenged habit of imputing authenticity to appearances.

> ...the worst sort of pride, that which values itself upon accidental advantages, not of its own achieving.
> **J.S. MILL 7**

We require parental support and guidance in order to establish ourselves. Simultaneously, our goal is to acquire values from preceding generations which lead to a noteworthy citizenry.

> The opportunity to contribute enduring excellence to civilization increases when morals and ethics prevail in the relationship between parents and their children
> **(RAYMOND B. CATTELL**, *Personal Communication).*

With integrity of morals between parents and offspring, there is no mistaking true development and self-reliance. Real achievement combines external wealth with internal virtue and character. Imbalance persists when we possess more than sufficient financial resources yet are chronically unhappy, addicted to self-destructive behavior and superficially involved with life. Excellence leads to increasing contentment and in this context, contentment is not unaspiring. It is the art of living well without a self-perpetuating assortment of artificial props.

Democracy in principle works well when a nations' citizens possess strong character. A nation plagued by a flood of lawmaking and a burdensome increase in lawyers reveals that valuable individual character is in short supply. Totalitarianism, by contrast, does not require individual strength of character as much as it demands unquestioning obedience. Today, the mass mind, in the name of democracy, is the dictator of whimsical and self-defeating national direction. We say "whimsical" because cultures led by the dictates of a mass mind become impoverished.

> The collapse of civilization has come about because we left the whole question of ethics to society.
>
> **A. SCHWEITZER 8**

American democracy will not survive with the freedoms of the last two centuries unless we create laws which place limits on the destructiveness of the mass mind. Furthermore, the ease and integrity of business practices in the past can no longer be relied upon to provide leadership for national interests. America's federal and trade deficits are not true problems; rather, they are symptoms of far graver problems developed over time.

As individual excellence declines, so does national excellence. Philosophies in favor of fairness and justice acknowledge that self-reliance, self-respect and initiative are the cornerstones of excellence. The kind of thinking necessary for equality undermines the desire for individual excellence.

> Equals too mutually imply one another...
>
> **DESCARTES 9**

At first sight the demand for equality seems to indicate a desire to rectify injustice. The ideological dilemma which seeks to lessen extremes of rich and poor fails to address the fact that advantages for some are achieved by honesty and hard work whereas advantages for others are the result of ill-gotten means (lying, cheating, stealing, profits from illegal drug sales, etc.). Endeavors which take money from those who operate against national interests and give that money to the poor are noble. Unfortunately, shrewd individuals of shady character are attracted to an illegal lifestyle and are wily enough to elude the vise of government. Equality in this context is a bizarre idea and only leads to shrewdness and slippery skill.

"Equality" and "liberty" are terms whose meanings are linked to specific contexts and these contexts change like the wind:

> Liberty, indeed, and the like specious names are their pretexts; but never did any man seek to enslave his fellows and secure dominion for himself, without using the very same words.   **TACITUS 10**

A sizable portion of the population falls within two categories: lazy or crafty. Many of these individuals are either on welfare or they cheat their neighbor and themselves. Both options are much too popular. Principles of hard work and integrity are not promoted by killing the incentive to work hard.

Excellence which provides evidence for qualitative change is of greater value than excellence whose outstanding characteristic is based upon quantity. For example, consider a ceiling-high stack of research with all the correct procedures, analyses and conclusions. Yet, a single piece of research, immediately translatable and penetratingly insightful, is of greater value than a stack of research (all of which is without procedural error) piled to the ceiling. True excellence is qualitative and rarely is it quantitative; mediocrity is generally quantitative and rarely is its emphasis qualitative. There is never an excess of Newtons, Darwins, Pasteurs, Edisons and Raymond B. Cattell's—gifted individuals who are oriented toward exceptionally high quality.

> The Newtons, Darwins, Pasteurs and Edisons are unusually stable, and capable of great patience and organized application to tasks. Deviation should be examined on its own merits, with a clear realization that society can suffer badly from too much of it— without dragging in obsolete superstitions about a bond of madness and genius.   **R.B. CATTELL 11**

Not only is it questionable whether our cultural environment allows and encourages greatness in rare individuals, many no longer desire the existence of exceptional and outstanding persons.

> Ordinary persons find no difference between men.
> **PASCAL 12**

> Originality is the one thing which unoriginal minds can-
> not feel the use of.   J.S. MILL 13

At a recent poll taken among college students, fifty percent
stated that their number one reason for being in college was to
make money. The primary goal is to learn the tricks of the trade:
how to acquire unlimited sums of money fast. The acquisition of
one million dollars does not offer proof for excellence. Excellence
is indicated when millionaires spend their money and use the
influence of their millions to enhance ethics and mental development. Some millionaires are rather dull and mediocre individuals.

Modern education makes an enduring contribution to civilization by assisting in the development of extraordinary individuals; modern education can also equalize thinking by stifling
the development of remarkable and far-reaching insights. What
passes for greatness in the minds of many, will soon be meaningless and obsolete.

> There is evidence quite recently that society tries to bend
> in everybody towards the mean
>   (RAYMOND B. CATTELL, *Personal Communication*).

> All this is to say that a civilization should entrust the job
> of education to its best minds—minds that are creative,
> comprehensive, gifted—wherever civilization can find
> men and women who possess such minds and are willing
> to dedicate their lives to the saving of a civilization which
> otherwise may destroy itself because it cannot under-
> stand itself.   D.E. LAWSON 14

We seek to understand how the anomaly of weirdness is
"admirable" while individuality is perceived as threatening? Is it
possible that one honest and intelligent human being makes it
more difficult for a majority to live in a mechanical and hollow
fashion? Throughout all grades, there is considerable discomfort
in the classroom when a student takes responsibility for his or her
thoughts. The media plays a major role in defining a range of
acceptable thoughts for a fluctuating mass mind. The dire need
for independent thinking is highly unpopular. "Popularity" today
lacks imagination and avoids taking responsibility for tomorrow.
If we doubt this, develop a solid platform, stick to it without
hemming and hawing and see if we get elected. Yet, this level of
unwavering conviction regarding issues of consequence is our

greatest need.

Today's teacher is more interested in pupils responding to cues than developing and responding according to conviction. A majority of the present generation of teachers concerned themselves with <u>parroting</u> their own instructors and thereby forfeited their opportunity for developing independent and valuable thinking. Education is a double edged sword: on the one hand, misguided education stimulates the passivity of mediocrity; on the other hand, education can foster independence of mind, creativity, honesty, a love of integrity and a willingness to seek out challenges rather than be seduced by momentary comforts.

> Myths are particularly likely to grow in the educational field because so many of our egalitarian hopes and aspirations are tied up with education; education seems to be the great equalizer, above all others.
>
> **H.J. EYSENCK 15**

We are in need of sound and comprehensive thinking. Those who are capable of this must summon all of their courage and take a stand. We need not fear competition because it does not exist at this level; we must share our thoughts in order to awaken Rip van Winkle—the country America. We would rather be awakened by sincere and concerned citizens who are able to point out the direction for restoring the greatness of America than be startled by the sound of tanks, guns and bombs, or discover that our country is for sale because it has weakened economically. Countries may very well be bought and sold on an international market in the next century. Far-fetched? Certainly, but not wholly impossible.

The danger of mediocrity as an acceptable standard is demonstrated by the inability to distinguish mediocrity from excellence (hard rock from Mozart, Tchaikovsky and Beethoven). We are so busy taking care of business and seeking out distractions, that the disappearance of quality from our life goes unnoticed. The farther we retreat to the beginnings of our country, the more elevated and valuable individual and collective thinking we find. People are starving for solid ideas and conversation worth remembering.

Those who lead financially comfortable and mediocre lives (unaware of changes in the spirit of the times), are enemies of excellence. Scripture informs us that to whom much is given, much is required. A contribution of excellence is worthy of esteem in future generations. Mediocrity says, "See, we are proof that we can live in an uncaring and selfish way—who needs to be concerned with tomorrow?" Should there arise a standard of genuine excellence in America, it will threaten the false security of mediocrity. From this perspective, excellence is the enemy.

> In fact, one of the main differences between great and ordinary people may be that great people pay close attention to their innate creativity and give careful consideration to what it offers.   **W. GLASSER 16**

At no time has the challenge to listen to our inner voice of creativity been greater. Excellence is closely related to the ability to develop realistic creativity. In the performing arts, the winner is the most natural.

Excellence primarily evolves in a milieu of progressive standards which emphasize quality. A particular state of mind achieves excellence, one which increases self-sufficiency and is self-legislative. Our accomplishments are not the result of luck or accident; the final products of noteworthy achievement are the sum of their high intention, ability and perseverance. In addition, we are challenged to look for the cause of personal experiences (irrespective of their nature), within ourselves. Enduring excellence requires an open mind, discipline and the desire to rise above the middle road. Individuals who have these qualities excel without much assistance from society. We should remove barriers and obstacles from those who create meaning and value.

Creative people are special, and when they are fortunate enough to be of strong character, they multiply the benefits of what they are given by one hundred fold. When certain "creative" people lack in character, we are cautioned to withhold support. Character in thought (intellectual honesty) is presently diminishing. Loyalty to principle constitutes the backbone of character. Mediocrity is recognized by the absence of backbone.

> For the virtuous, being steadfast in themselves [in view of their virtue], remain steadfast towards each other also and they neither ask others to do what is bad nor do they themselves do such things for others, but one might say that they even prevent such things from being done...   **ARISTOTLE 17**

REFERENCES

1. Cattell, R.B. (1933). *Psychology and social progress.* London: Daniel. Page 81.

2. *The Holy Bible.* London: Oxford University Press.

3. Descartes. Volume 31. Page 41.

4. Spinoza, Ethics IV. Quoted in *Great treasury of western thought* (1977). Eds. Mortimer J. Adler & Charles Van Doren. New York and London: R.R. Bowker. Page 297.

5. Tillich, P. (1952). *Courage to be.* New Haven, Connecticut: Yale University Press. Page 73.

6. Revel, Jean-Francois (1983). *How democracies perish.* Garden City, NY: Doubleday. Pages 12-13.

7. Mill, J.S. (1869, 1970). *The subjection of women.* Cambridge, Massachusetts and London: The M.I.T. Press. Page 81.

8. Schweitzer, (1947). *Albert Schweitzer: an anthology.* Edited by Charles R. Joy. Boston: Beacon Press. Page 195.

9. Descartes. Volume 31. Page 8.

10. Tacitus. Volume 15. Page 290.

11. Cattell, R.B. (1972). *A new morality from science: Beyonism.* New York: Pergamon. Page 451.

12. Pascal. Volume 33. Page 173.

13. Mill, J.S. Volume 43. Page 298.

14. Lawson, D.E. (1961). *Wisdom and education.* Carbondale: Southern

Illinois Press. Page 73.

15. Eysenck, H.J. (1973). *The inequality of man.* London: Temple Smith. Page 155.

16. Glasser, W. (1984). *Take effective control of your life.* New York: Harper & Row. Page 227.

17. Aristotle (1975). *The nicomachean ethics.* Dordrecht-Holland and Boston: D. Reidel. Page 151.

CHAPTER TEN

MORALE vs. APATHY

Never before in the history of America has apathy (non-involvement) been so prevalent. An oft-repeated defeatist view claims, "There is nothing we can do to make a difference." Even when there is involvement, rarely does it strengthen our country. Involvement too often seeks narrow self-pursuit: for example, political action committees, homosexual rights, feminist rights, abortion versus pro-life rights, misguided libertarian notions (which frequently focus on freedom without responsibility), and the local golf club! To be involved is insufficient; mere activity falls short of qualifying as "experience." The larger question remains, "with what am I involved and what is its value?"

> ...a man must learn how one thing is a consequence of other things, and when one thing follows from one thing, and when it follows from several collectively.
>
> **EPICTETUS 1**

Whatever the problems and suffering of a group or nation, they result from individual attitudes, persuasions, choices and behavior. For example, several factors precede the outcome of an unwanted pregnancy. For fifteen years we have watched placard-carrying protestors exhibit strong emotion in pro and anti-abortion camps. Both groups claim rights. Debates have been carried on; bombs have been detonated in abortion clinics. Despite all the expended energy and noise, there have been no noticeable ideological changes or progress since abortion has become a public concern. Pro and anti-abortion debates camouflage a greater issue: the question of whether life is worth living without minimal standards. In the near future, American citizens will be required to establish standards for defining a life worth living.

If we doubt there is a morale crisis, consider the significant drug usage in America during the past three decades. For a sizable portion of the population, life is not worth living without habitual recourse to a mesmerized state of mind, aided by an external agent. People live for drugs, and if drugs were suddenly unavailable, many would prefer instantaneous death.

It is difficult to gauge accurately the total effect of the drug menace on society. Foreign governments and civilians, not to mention thousands of small and big-time drug dealers in America, profit greatly from habitual drug consumption. Those who "prosper" by illegal activities aspire to live in grand style, oblivious of the drain on our national resources.

> Never yet has any one exercised for good ends the power
> obtained by crime.   TACITUS 2

There are at least two explanations for habitual drug usage: mental inadequacy and long-term apathy. Drugs impair our minds and routine drug usage is indicative of inadequate mental assurance. A viable mind does not rely upon drug-induced stimulation. Americans who on rare occasion flirt with drugs represent only a small fraction of drug consumption. Relentless daily consumption accounts for the magnitude of the present drug market to the tune of billions of dollars. How is it possible that this state of affairs exists in a country which offers so much of value to live for? H.G. Wells wrote at the end of World War II that it would henceforth be difficult to make rational sense of people's thinking and behavior. Well's assessment has even greater validity today.

During the 1960's, widespread belief that money could solve our problems fostered false hopes. Better homes, automobiles and jobs would provide incentive for quality living. Wrong. There are any number of mentally inadequate individuals carrying $100 bills, driving costly cars and living in extravagant homes. Materialism is a short-sighted yardstick with which to measure the quality of life. Yet this concept recently has become a driving force. With lots of money, we can afford high-class prostitutes, drink fine liquor, smoke imported tobacco, snort cocaine and take frequent trips to gambling casinos. Having more money than is needed to live comfortably does not inherently advance the virtuous and quality aspects of most people's lives.

Virtue is viewed as peculiar and unprofitable. The present lack of virtue is alarming. Historically, religion demanded virtue in people. In addition to religion we must look to schools, homes, movies, peer pressure and scientific morality to re-establish the significance of virtue.

A not uncommon view is that living has become so frivolous that the next generation can be expected to adopt a similar life of frivolity; therefore, why introduce more infants into such a world? Previously, upon becoming pregnant, a woman asked herself what kind of child might be born. Today many women take a sober look at reality (at themselves and the man by whom they were impregnated) only to rush off to the abortion clinic. In the face of a steady demand for one million abortions annually, what are the arguments against motherhood? The incentives to have an abortion appear to outweigh the reasons against it.

At best we can explain away twenty percent of unwanted pregnancies on the basis of mishap and bad luck. Accidents do occur, but nature is not that inconsistent. How do we explain the other eighty percent of abortions? Ignorance and incorrect usage of birth control methods? If ignorance of birth control measures suffices to explain away the incredible number of unwanted pregnancies (with Planned Parenthood clinics everywhere), we sorely need serious educational reform in our attitude toward sexuality. The outrageous increase of unwanted pregnancies points to a cult of sexual irresponsibility. When we consider the expectations and demands for sexual experience combined with one million abortions annually, we must conclude that America is schizoid in her sexual behavior and beliefs. We are not only inept users of birth control measures, but more important, we are immature in our approach toward sex.

Ironically, the number of unwanted pregnancies has increased with the ease of access to Planned Parenthood clinics across America. When the "cure" increases the problem, something is woefully wrong. Given the facts, it is difficult to arrive at a coherent understanding of present sexual attitudes and practices in America in light of a high abortion rate.

Pro-lifers believe that abortions are immoral. In accepting belief in a soul, how do clinical abortions, miscarriage (abortion by natural causes), and suicide (the deliberate abortion of a life no longer worth living) differ?

A thorough investigation which studies the demographics of

abortion is in order. Once we identify the approximate age range when thirty to forty percent of women have an abortion, the public should be alerted. The high risk age group must be informed that they are prime candidates for an unwanted pregnancy and abortion. Pro and anti-abortion resources can share in the task. Both camps could pool their resources rather than continue to waste time, money and energy fighting one another (without effecting any shift in a troublesome situation). Whatever the causes of an incredibly high abortion rate, revoking the legality of abortion will not remedy the factors which lead to unwanted pregnancies. A greater emphasis must be placed on measures such as demographic awareness, birth control education and honest communication between partners so that the incidence of abortion can be reduced or eliminated.

Rampant abortions provide evidence for serious moral problems. With a minimal intelligent effort to redress our attitudes towards sexual relations, unwanted pregnancies could rapidly decline. In view of recent major changes (birth control, misuse of freedom, the de-emphasis of sincere and honest living), whether pro or anti-abortion, maturity in our sexual attitudes and behavior is needed.

Certain modes of behavior are more effectively governed by national precepts of morality, peer pressure, and cultural standards, than by law. Noticeably, the aforementioned three factors carry little weight at this time.

> ...here the great art lies, to discern in what the law is to bid restraint and punishment, and in what things persuasion only is to work.   **MILTON 3**

Poor communication between sexual partners leads to unwanted pregnancies. Teen-age sex is common; even eleven and twelve years olds are sexually active. What will these youngsters do for an "encore" when they are thirty, forty and fifty years of age? Is life and school so boring and unattractive that teen-agers find it necessary to seek out sex in order to feel alive? Today's younger generation is unconvinced that life is worthwhile, so many pursue drugs, sex and the escapism of television.

> If you deliver a nation to amusement and sensuality, if all of its power and courage is drained in order to deter thought, who will defend it against warlike neighbors?
> **MADAME DE STAEL 4**

Predictably, a morale crisis is preceded by the lack of respect for independent thought. A major source for developing and sustaining a critical mind is the reading of books in the following areas: history, autobiographies and biographies, the classics, science, philosophy, theology, political science and literature. Many people consider serious reading boring.

A book should be an ice-pick to break up the frozen sea within us. **FRANZ KAFKA 5**

Much of the required reading in the social sciences of academia does not inspire; many minds with potential are turned off, never to recover. The kind of reading material which develops an independent and versatile mind is rarely included in the present curriculum or read by the majority of today's teachers. How many college students have read some of Plato, Pascal, Nietzsche, Bacon, Montaigne, Kierkegaard, Gibbon, Goethe, Samuel Johnson, Boswell and John Stuart Mill? These writers command language and stimulate at the same time. Once an appetite for solid reading material is awakened, it rarely dies. Reading worthwhile non-fiction activates mental development and leads to serious craving for challenging and creative ideas, a longing which rivals an addict's crave for drug stimulation.

Such as are thy habitual thoughts, such also will be the character of thy mind; for the soul is dyed by the thoughts. **MARCUS AURELIUS 6**

Exactly how does reading contribute to morale? First of all, only a quiet mind can absorb material worth reading. Secondly, reading increases our attention span—the ability to focus and concentrate. Thirdly, reading offers an expanded conceptual world, a contribution which lends itself to identity-formation (awareness of who I am and who you are), a standard of values and a basis for intelligent choices. How we spend our time individually does affect national morale. In addition, it is not an excess of bad thoughts which poses the greatest difficulty; it is the lack of elevated and virtuous thinking which leads to apathy. Without striving for dignity, honor and selflessness, life becomes a downward spiral. Apathy is simply a symptom of a life lacking quality.

It is natural for the mind to believe and for the will to

> love; so that, for want of true objects, they must attach
> themselves to false. **PASCAL 7**

A plural society like America can accommodate false objects provided there are also true objects. We must seriously question whether or not sufficient true objects (those capable of evoking nationwide involvement) can be rediscovered. What do we mean when we say, "We are proud to be American?" The crowd roars, "Freedom, freedom of speech and the freedom to pursue whatever turns us on." And the echo comes back, "Freedom to take drugs, freedom to engage sexually (with and without mutual consent), disregarding emotional development and long-term effects on future generations; freedom to deceive and even to commit crimes if they serve to remove perceived obstacles." Once upon a time freedom included the freedom to walk anywhere unmolested, freedom to trust the spoken word, freedom to think and freedom to make an enduring contribution to a rapidly expanding country. Freedom presumed a love of honor and truth; today, it often means the opportunity to waste life.

> For—and this is the verdict of everyone—if the world
> only consisted of lifeless beings, or even consisted partly
> of living, but yet irrational beings, the existence of such
> a world would have no worth whatever, because there
> would exist in it no being with the least conception of
> what worth is. **KANT 8**

A common interpretation of Christianity (mostly based on grace) erodes the very necessary idea of being worthy. For example, the congregation rejoices when a man or woman gives up a fifty year habit of debauchery to be unreservedly welcomed into the fold. This story does more to demoralize than promote virtue. It teaches us to flirt with chance, to experience life treacherously (provided we are "saved" before the midnight hour). Teaching value in last-minute grace does little to promote long-term morality. The scriptures are full of examples which seem to teach value in last-minute grace. On the practical level, this notion is devilish. It destroys the value of standards. This example alone illustrates the necessity for separation of church and state. Our forefathers witnessed endless tomfoolery in Europe (which lasted for centuries), when church and state commingled. Grace is good and necessary; in the aforementioned context, it makes for bad philosophy.

It is next to impossible to sustain morale in an atmosphere of deception. Morale thrives when mutual respect and dignity prevail in addition to the fulfillment of our basic needs (food, clothing and shelter). Morale is reflected in the cohesion of society, a cohesion which cuts through financial status, sex, race and creed. The level of morale reflects the integrity of society.

> ...for it is only inexperienced people who suppose that it is easy to deceive innocence; existence is very profound, and it is in fact the easiest thing for the shrewd to fool the shrewd...   **KIERKEGAARD 9**

It is impossible to maintain morale when lying, cheating and trickery are the order of the day. It can not be disputed that America maintained noteworthy morale until the assassination of John F. Kennedy and the Vietnam War. Ever thereafter, we as a nation continue to suffer from an ever growing loss of morale, which results in the weakening of individual and national character.

Guilt, innocence, morality and inner security are interdependent. A complete loss of innocence (incorrigibility) is generally coupled with immorality and leads to the inability to experience guilt. The alerting feedback of guilt, as a protecting radar, is no longer available. Small wonder we become insecure as individuals or collectively. During the past one hundred years, our relationship with guilt reflects a tendency to extremes. In Freud's cultural milieu at the turn of the 19th century, a slight deviation provoked a crushing sense of guilt. Guilt response was far too sensitive and burdensome. Today we have effectively destroyed innocence and are unable to feel guilt precisely when we ought to experience it.

It is true that innocence and naivete go hand in hand during the developmental years of our lives. Our challenge is to become less naive as we advance in years without selling our innocence. To be exceedingly naive means utter vulnerability in the company of shrewd, unethical and warped individuals. Now innocence is prized, being the one virtue which keeps life from becoming unmercifully sordid and stale.

Technological breakthroughs will not ipso facto restore the recent erosion of morale. There was a time when technological advances were received with national rejoicing. As a nation we applauded the first man walking on the moon, and we continue to deify medical discoveries. This deification silently waits for the medicine god (doctors and medical researchers) to come up with a solution which renders the human immunodeficiency virus (HIV) harmless. Peter Duesberg, molecular biologist at UC Berkeley, believes that HIV is not the cause of AIDS. He and other noted authorities recognize in AIDS a habitual disregard for the safeguarding of immunity in the history of the patient. Duesberg believes that a major problem precedes the damage done by HIV: a deadly breakdown in immune function or weak immune function to begin with. HIV is an opportunistic virus which exacerbates an already weak immunity.

> If you find a microbe or a virus in a disease, that doesn't prove it is the cause of the disease.   **Duesberg 10**

One of the reasons why it is so difficult to assess the range of damage from HIV may be attributed to the wide innate variation in immune response from individual to individual. How is it that some heavy smokers live past eighty without a major smoking-related disease? The resistance to the harmful effects of smoking are stronger in that individual (prior to lighting the first cigarette) than in other smokers. Likewise, it may be possible for two people to lead a similar lifestyle, yet one dies of AIDS while the other appears to remain unaffected. Why? A significant difference in immune efficiency could explain the dilemma. However, this is potentially misleading: the survivor may remain unaffected for several years and suddenly (within three or four months) capitulate to an active HIV.

Just as the immune system breaks down because it has been over-exposed to diseases and viruses, when contradictory and foolish ideas repeatedly enter the human mind, it also is rendered incapable of producing logical and empirically sound ideas. The immune system must be nurtured in order to remain strong; the human mind must occasionally inculcate worthwhile thoughts in order to develop and remain capable of sound thinking.

Education can be extremely helpful, but . . . it must be the right kind of education. For many, the experience of education is irremediably damaging due to the near impossibility to correct goofy ideas and bad habits acquired in the course of higher education. The time has come when we must insist upon a well-rounded and integrated educational system.

> ...when the human mind has once despaired of discovering truth, everything begins to languish. Hence men

turn aside into pleasant controversies and discussions,
and into a sort of wandering over subjects rather than
sustain any rigorous investigation.　　**F. BACON 11**

Even if a discovery nullifies the effects of HIV, our AIDS
problem is not ended.　Only strict concentration on the exact
determination of that which weakens the immune system will
eliminate the AIDS threat to our future.

Compassion for those afflicted with AIDS has gone
beyond a stage conducive to competition. The general
proposition of a Beyondist perspective is that inner
group morality is the basis of survival. By letting
immoral cultures go down the drain (like Sodom and
Gomorrah), morality survives with moral groups. Today, postwar Japan and West Germany provide evidence of comparatively good survival. It is as if morality is a thing in and of itself which survives through
various happenings within and among groups. The Beyondist position insists upon awareness of competition
among groups. About fifty percent of Americans think
morality is only Judaic-Christian, whereas there are
other systems of morality: Islam, Taoism, Buddhism
and Beyondism. The weakness of Christianity in present American usage is that it increases all kinds of
inefficient living. As part of its preaching, it regards the
extension of national resources to the incompetent and
immoral as acceptable. The Beyondist position insists
upon the maintenance of competition among groups.
Compassion for AIDS victims and similar departures
from moral standards have reached the point of weakening national strength.
It is essential that the results of a lifestyle should pay off
in effects to holders of that lifestyle. People should not
automatically assume they have a right to demand from
others a remedy for their departure from a healthy
lifestyle. Today's compassion is blind to the acceptance
of the reality of a wrathful Jehovah. Groups recoup their
morale only through destruction. People have deluded
themselves into believing that compassion for those
afflicted with AIDS is the moral thing to show
　　(RAYMOND B. CATTELL, *Personal Communication).*

Laws of nature are generally resilient in allowing some
deviation and error; they will not accommodate perpetual and

flagrant violation. There is a conflict of interest between the freedom to do as we please and limits imposed by nature. For example, in a society where the majority are in good health most of the time, we conceivably could kiss fifty different people annually without weakening our immune system. We do not live in a healthy society. When our immune system has to fight off a succession of viruses and diseases (particularly with frequent recourse to the artificial help of modern medicine), it is not surprising that abusers of the body's natural immunity Acquire Immune Deficiency Syndrome. Medicines are powerful and rather effective in the short term; excessive and habitual use of strong medicines weakens their effect in the long term. A vicious cycle comprises three factors. Exposure to foreign substances calls for the aid of modern medicine, the dependence upon which weakens our natural immune system. This process over a period of many years culminates in an immune crisis at which time HIV multiplies and death is imminent.

> In times during which no obstacles to sexual satisfaction existed, such as, may be during the decline of the civilizations of antiquity, love became worthless, life became empty, and strong reaction-formations were necessary before the indispensable emotional value of love could be recovered.   **FREUD 12**

Anybody may choose to die but nobody has the freedom to live without standards of behavior. Millions of people live with low standards; this is not freedom. We can not say, "We have the freedom to be prisoners," because we were not born to be prisoners. The price for individual freedom is individual moral responsibility.

Indisputably, nine out of ten people have a woefully limited understanding of history and the development of freedom over the past two hundred years. If we do not respect history, neither can we understand the necessity of securing freedom for future generations. The implications of this are far more grave than is readily evident. For example, if our experience of sincerity, sacrifice and dignity (common characteristics at the time a strong America was created), is limited or nonexistent, it is next to impossible to understand the meaning of losing "cherished" freedoms. Only a generation of sleepy citizens lacking true objects of attachment and having abandoned the search for value and meaning, feel no guilt in aiding the downfall of a great nation.

It is no accident that morale and morality have the same
root; for correlational research across national cultures
shows that individual moral levels and group morale
levels are closely bound (Cattell and Gorsuch, 1965). Of
all factors contributing to group survival, preventing
cultural breakdown, and avoiding dissolution into scattered primitive brutishness, that morale which goes
with the virtues of unselfishness, considerateness,
honesty, loyalty and love of one's neighbor is probably
the most important.   **R.B. CATTELL 13**

During those periods of our history when high morale
prevailed, citizens proud to be American were cognizant of individual contributions to the nation and of collective strength of
character. They experienced feelings of self-worth, self-sacrifice
and devotion to truth and honesty. Substance, not appearances
and artificial props, supported national pride. Any number of
individuals today are proud to be Americans for the wrong
reasons. Their pride hates innocence, desires idleness and
squanders money.

Deeply-rooted apathy has a history whose origin is subtle
and resists explanation. Once apathy is firmly established, the
return to morality through healing and mending is possible only
with harsh measures, which are strongly resisted. Sustained
apathy is maintained by the refusal to seek out competition for
the purpose of development, and is but a short distance from
surrender to antagonistic forces which break down to suicide.

Inactivity, unaspiringness, absence of desire, are a more
fatal hindrance to improvement than any misdirection
of energy...   **J.S. MILL 14**

Morale is like happiness in that both are products of individual and collective lifestyles. Today's world is globally intertwined; survival depends upon our combined efforts to create a
world in which competition, cooperation and sanity predominate.
A mature conscience does not escape into isolation and intention-
ally look the other way with the aim of ignoring problems. Efforts
to seclude ourselves in cozy environments while pretending that
ignorance, suffering and abuses are other peoples' problems,
contribute in a major way to the present morale crisis.

Modern technology provides great resources; yet, the re-
source of thinking is diminishing. For example, what does it
mean to give money to religious organizations: are we purchas-

ing lottery tickets in hope of a better life after death by supporting questionable crafters of religion? Giving is wonderful (it is more blessed to give than to receive), but . . . in a fast, bureaucratic world, many of our gifts merely purchase debauchery for the recipients. As stalwart citizens, let us give responsibly and require to see immediate fruits of our giving, particularly in matters pertaining to religion. With this approach we are able to control when giving is a blessing for the recipient and when giving becomes a curse (far more often than we are willing to admit), in which latter case we ought to cease giving.

A crisis in morale is a crisis in accountability. Citizens and, more important, those in positions of authority, must be held accountable. Immunity from accountability in high office stands in need of rethinking and requires new and equitable guidelines. Hiding behind exemption from accountability is not true leadership. This is illustrated by our present state of affairs about which we read in today's newspaper and which was occurring more than 1600 years ago:

> ...industry at home, just government without, a mind free in deliberation, addicted neither to crime nor to lust. Instead of these, we have luxury and avarice, poverty in the state, opulence among citizens; we laud riches, we follow laziness; there is no difference made between the good and the bad; all the rewards of virtue are got possession of by intrigue. And no wonder, when every individual consults only for his own good, when ye are the slaves of pleasure at home, and, in public affairs, of money and favour, no wonder that an onslaught is made upon the unprotected republic.   **CATO 15**

REFERENCES

1. Epictetus. Volume 12. Page 112.

2. Tacitus. Volume 15. Page 197.

3. Milton. Volume 32. Page 394.

4. de Stael, Madame (1964). *On politics, literature and national character.* Garden City, New York: Doubleday. Page 255.

5. "Franz Kafka: Hunt the jackdaw." London: The Economist Newspaper LTD. "The Economist" 16-22 January 1988, Page 88.

6. Aurelius, Marcus. Volume 12. Page 271.

7. Pascal. Volume 33. Page 186.

8. Kant. Volume 42. Page 594.

9. Kierkegaard (1843, 1941). *Fear and trembling.* Princeton, NJ: Princeton University Press. Page 149.

10. Shurkin, Joel N. "The aids bebate: another view." Los Angeles Times 18 January 1988. Part II, Page 4.

11. Bacon, F. Volume 30. Page 116.

12. Freud, S. (1959). *Collected papers.* New York: Basic Books. Volume IV, Page 213.

13. Cattell, R.B. (1972). *A new morality from science.* New York: Pergamon. Page 100.

14. Mill, J.S. Volume 43. Page 348.

15. Augustine. Volume 18. Page 218.

INDEX

Send me _____ copies of **WISDOM FOR OUR TIME.** Enclosed is $12.95 plus $2.00 postage and handling. California residents add 6% state sales tax (San Diego county residents – 7%). Order from:

Quality Life Publishing Company
11727 Invierno Drive
San Diego, California 92124

Name _____

Address _____

City _____

State _____ Zip Code _____

Please allow four to six weeks for delivery.

Two public speaking presentations are offered
by the author for a fee:

HOW IMPORTANT IS YOUR LIFE?

CAN AMERICAN FREEDOM SURVIVE?

Address inquiries to Daniel W. Gudeman,
Quality Life Publishing Company,
11727 Invierno Drive, San Diego, California 92124

Send me _____ copies of **WISDOM FOR OUR TIME.** Enclosed is $12.95 plus $2.00 postage and handling. California residents add 6% state sales tax (San Diego county residents – 7%). Order from:

Quality Life Publishing Company
11727 Invierno Drive
San Diego, California 92124

Name _____

Address _____

City _____

State _____ Zip Code _____

Please allow four to six weeks for delivery.

Two public speaking presentations are offered
by the author for a fee:

HOW IMPORTANT IS YOUR LIFE?

CAN AMERICAN FREEDOM SURVIVE?

Address inquiries to Daniel W. Gudeman,
Quality Life Publishing Company,
11727 Invierno Drive, San Diego, California 92124